TABLE OF CONTENTS

STRUCTURE OF REVELATION: 4 PARTS AND 5 SECTIONS (IN THE 4TH PART)

Rev. 1   **PART 1** John's **CALLING** to prophesy about the end times: John gives specific truths about Jesus' majesty—truths that form the way he prophesies about the end times, and that are meant to equip us.

Rev. 2-3   **PART 2** Jesus gives **SEVEN LETTERS** to seven churches: The instructions Jesus gives to these seven churches about overcoming sin give us practical insight into what we too must overcome today.

Rev. 4-5   **PART 3** Jesus takes the **SCROLL**: The scroll represents the title deed of the earth and Jesus' battle plan to cleanse the whole earth in preparation for His rule. Jesus' battle plan is seen in the events of Revelation 6-22.

Rev. 6-22   **PART 4** Jesus' **BATTLE PLAN** is written in the scroll and includes the Great Tribulation judgments against the Babylon religion and the Antichrist's empire. In these chapters, Jesus reveals His main story line of love to cleanse the earth of evil. His battle plan is described in *five chronological sections* describing the judgment events, each followed by an *angelic explanation.*

The five chronological sections tell us what happens to the Antichrist's followers in the twenty-one judgment events (seven seals, seven trumpets, and seven bowls), which intensify in severity as they unfold.

The five angelic explanations function as a parenthesis, putting the story line "on pause." They answer questions arising from the chronological sections: Why is God's wrath so severe? What will happen to us? Angels explain to John what will happen to God's people, including what Jesus will do to help the saints and what the Antichrist will do to persecute them.

Book of
Revelation
Study Guide
NKJV

Notes by Mike Bickle

IHOP.org
MikeBickle.org

forerunner
PUBLISHING

Second edition, January 2010
The Book of Revelation Study Guide
With Notes by Mike Bickle

Published by Forerunner Publishing
International House of Prayer
3535 E. Red Bridge Road
Kansas City, MO 64137

forerunnerpublishing@ihop.org

IHOP.org
MikeBickle.org

ISBN: 978-0-9823262-0-6

Produced by Misty Edwards and Nick Syrett
Cover design by Adam Grason

"I would like to thank Nick Syrett for initiating this project and for the countless hours that he poured into it at every stage of its development." - Mike Bickle

Rev. 6   *Chronological section #1:* The SEAL JUDGMENTS against the kingdom of darkness

Rev. 7   *Angelic explanation #1:* the saints receive PROTECTION from judgments and from falling away from the faith

Rev. 8-9   *Chronological section #2:* the TRUMPET JUDGMENTS against the Antichrist's empire

Rev. 10-11 *Angelic explanation #2:* the saints receive DIRECTION by the great increase of prophetic ministry

Rev. 11:15-19 *Chronological section #3:* the SECOND COMING PROCESSION and the rapture of the Church

The seventh and last trumpet (1 Cor. 15:52; 1 Thes. 4:16; Rev. 10:7): Jesus will replace all governmental leaders on earth in a hostile takeover. He will lead a royal procession across the earth. He will first travel across the sky to rapture the saints (every eye will see Him; Rev. 1:7), then through the land of Edom (modern-day Jordan; Isa. 63:1-6; Hab. 3:12) destroying His enemies, then to Jerusalem and the Mount of Olives (Zech. 14:2-5).

Rev. 12-14 *Angelic explanation #3:* Antichrist's violent CONFRONTATION against the saints and all that is good in society requires that all his evil governments be replaced

Rev. 15-16 *Chronological section #4:* the BOWL JUDGMENTS destroy evil infrastructures in society (Ps. 2:9)

Rev. 17-18 *Angelic explanation #4:* the SEDUCTION of society by Babylon's evil religion will permeate and infiltrate every social structure, requiring that Babylon be totally destroyed

Rev. 19-20 *Chronological section #5:* Jesus' TRIUMPHAL ENTRY to Jerusalem (Rev. 19:11-21:8)

Rev. 21-22 *Angelic explanation #5:* the RESTORATION of all things (Acts 3:21; Rev. 21:9-22:5)

INTRODUCTION BY MIKE BICKLE

My goal in this book is to provide a simple road map of the book of Revelation so that anyone can understand its straightforward message. The Spirit gave the Scripture, including Revelation, to be understood by all who love Jesus.

I greatly value the benefit of biblical scholarship. However, we do not need a doctorate in theology to understand the Bible's basic message. The majority of people throughout history were uneducated. Yet, God intended them to understand the Scripture, including the book of Revelation.

Revelation is first and foremost a book that reveals the glory of Jesus as one who is fully God and fully Man (Rev. 1:1). Therefore, its message is not primarily about future events; these are a secondary theme. It is first about the Man behind the plan. It is first about Jesus and His return to take leadership of the nations and restore the earth.

I am regularly asked if I believe the end of the world will happen in my lifetime. People are surprised when I answer that the Bible makes clear that the world will never end but will continue forever (Ps. 37:29; 78:69; 104:5; 105:10-11; 125:1-2; 1 Chr. 23:25; 28:8; Isa. 60:21; Ezek. 37:25; Joel 3:20).

> *Like the earth which He has established forever. (Ps. 78:69)*

> *You who laid the foundations of the earth, so that it should not be moved forever. (Ps. 104:5)*

Some talk about the end of the world. At Jesus' second coming, He does not bring an end to this world; He brings an end to this age. The government of the nations in this age is influenced by demonic activity. In the age to come, Jesus will govern the nations without any demonic interference.

The book of Revelation is a glorious love story. It is not a doomsday prophecy about the world coming to an end. It is God's plan to usher in a new beginning for the world. Yes, the birth of a baby is the end of a pregnancy, but it is mostly about the beginning of a new life. The book of Revelation describes the end of the dark night of Satan's oppression of human history and the dawning of a new day of Jesus' glory and love for the whole earth.

I do not ask anyone to accept my views; rather I urge you to boldly challenge all the ideas that you read in this study guide. Refuse any that you cannot clearly see in Scripture for yourself. I urge you to be like the Bereans who searched the Scriptures to see if the things that Paul said were so (Acts 17:10-11).

The most controversial point in this study guide is found in my conviction that the Church will go through the Tribulation in great victory and power. This differs from the popular pretribulation rapture view that teaches that the Church will be raptured at any minute.

The Bible does teach that the Church will be raptured, but it will be raptured at the end of the Tribulation, not before it starts. I honor the godliness of many who hold the pretribulation rapture view, but I see it as a serious mistake that will leave many unprepared. We can agree to disagree in a spirit of meekness and honor.

The Church will be raptured after it goes through the Tribulation in great victory and revival. Jesus has planned for His Church to be on the earth at that time to partner with Him as He judges the worldwide oppression of the Antichrist.

The end-time Church will be engaged in a dramatic prayer movement which will release the most powerful justice movement in history. The great oppression and injustices of the Antichrist's worldwide empire will be completely overthrown at Jesus' return.

We need not fear God's judgments described in the book of Revelation. They do not happen to us as helpless victims of the Antichrist but are released through us as participants who follow Jesus' leadership. The Great Tribulation is primarily about God's judgment against the Antichrist's empire.

Its secondary theme is the persecution of the saints by the Antichrist. There are only twelve verses in the book of Revelation that directly mention the persecution of the saints (Rev. 6:9-11; 11:7; 12:17; 13:7, 15; 16:6; 17:6; 18:24; 19:2; 20:4). These twelve verses make up only about 3 percent of the 403 verses of Revelation.

The accumulation of all the prayers of the saints through history along with the acceleration of their prayers in the end times will be used under Jesus' leadership to release God's judgments against the Antichrist's empire that will oppress the nations. The saints are only to pray for these judgments after the Tribulation begins and only on the reprobate who take the mark of the Beast signifying their final rejection of the gospel and their oppression of the saints.

Then another angel . . . stood at the altar. And he was given much incense, that he should offer it with the prayers of all the saints upon the golden altar . . . And the smoke of the incense, with the prayers of the saints, ascended before God from the angel's hand. Then the angel took the censer, filled it with fire from the altar, and threw it to the earth. (Rev. 8:3-5)

The Spirit is raising up a mighty end-time prayer and worship movement (Lk. 18:7-8; Mt. 21:13; 25:1-13; Rev. 5:8; 6:9-11; 8:3-5; 9:13; 14:18; 16:7; 18:6; 22:17; Isa. 19:20-22; 24:14-16; 25:9; 26:8-9; 27:2-5, 13; 30:18-19; 42:10-13; 43:26; 51:11; 52:8; 62:6-7; Jer. 31:7; 51:8; Joel 2:12-17, 32; Zeph. 2:1-3; Ps. 102:17-20; 122:6; 149:6-9; Zech. 8:20-23; 10:1; 12:10; 13:9).

As the book of Acts describes the power of the Holy Spirit that was released through the early church, so the book of Revelation describes the power of the Holy Spirit that will be released through the end-time Church. I, therefore, refer to Revelation as the end-time book of Acts.

As Moses released God's judgments on Pharaoh by prayer (Ex. 7-12), so the end-time Church will release the tribulation judgments on the Antichrist, the end-time Pharaoh, through unified prayer.

Revelation is a canonized prayer manual that informs us of the specific ways in which Jesus will manifest His power through the praying Church. For example, imagine hundreds of millions of believers with a unified prayer focus because they know the sequence in which the trumpet judgments will unfold. We all know that the fourth trumpet will come after the third trumpet, and so on!

Jesus will express His love in the nations by releasing His judgments against the Antichrist's empire. His judgments will remove everything that hinders love. He will overthrow all the evil systems that perpetuate injustice and oppression.

KEEPING THE WORDS OF THE PROPHECY

The Church throughout history is promised a blessing to any who do three things: read it (includes studying it); hear it (includes agreeing with it); and keep it (includes acting on it).

> *Blessed is he who reads and those who hear the words of this prophecy, and keep those things which are written in it. (Rev. 1:3)*

> *I am coming quickly! Blessed is he who keeps the words of the prophecy of this book . . . I (angel) am your fellow servant, and . . . of those who keep the words of this book. (Rev. 22:7-9)*

This promise will have its greatest fulfillment in the generation in which the Lord returns, because only those on earth during the events prophesied by John are in a position to keep the prophecy to the fullest extent. Believers through history have kept the prophecy in the sense of obeying the commands that Jesus gave in the prophecy, such as abstaining from immorality (Rev. 2:14, 20). Keeping the prophecy in its fullest sense means to participate with Jesus in the unfolding of the holy drama described in the prophecy itself.

The Church "**keeps the prophecy**" by acting on it in various ways:

- By **obeying** Jesus: the saints will be empowered in their faith as the thirty truths about Jesus' majesty and ministry (in Rev. 1-3) touch their hearts.

- By **saying** the main truths set forth in "the prophecy."

- By **praying** for the release of judgments against the Antichrist as described in "the prophecy." The saints are only to pray for these judgments after the Tribulation begins, and only for judgment on the reprobate who take the mark of the Beast, thereby signifying their final rejection of the gospel and their oppression of the saints.

PART 1: Revelation 1

John's **CALLING** to prophesy about the end times: In this chapter John gives specific truths about Jesus' majesty—truths that form the way he prophesies about the end times, and that are meant to equip us.

REV. 1   **v.1 Revelation**: the book is called the *Revelation of Jesus* because it reveals His heart and leadership. The Father's primary purpose in giving this book was to reveal Jesus' majesty. It is secondarily a book about events in the end times.

In Revelation 1-3 Jesus highlighted thirty distinct descriptions of His majesty and ministry. It is the most complete picture of Him in Scripture, giving us greater insight into **who He is** (how He thinks and feels) and **what He does** in preparing the nations for His return. He is seen as the Son of Man who leads the Church through history as the *Prophet, Priest, and King*. Jesus gave us these insights into His majesty and ministry to form the way we pray, prophesy, and serve Him. Thus, we will prophesy about the end times with a right spirit (tenderness and confidence) instead of a wrong spirit (harshness and fear). As the book unfolds, He is revealed more fully to all the nations at the end of the age (Rev. 19-22) as the *Bridegroom, King, and Judge.*

v.3 Blessed: blessing is promised to those who do three things with the book of Revelation prophecy: **read it** (includes studying it); **hear it** (includes agreeing with it); and **keep it** (includes acting on it) in three ways. *See page 9.*

v.5 Jesus: referred to here by three messianic titles from Psalm 89.

v.5 faithful witness: in His earthly ministry, He revealed the truth and stood for it regardless of the cost (Jn. 3:11; 5:31-32; 8:13-14; 8:18, 23; 18:37).

v.5 firstborn: He is in the position of a firstborn heir of God's kingdom. This does not mean He was the first one born, but is the first in authority. He is the firstborn from the dead because He is the first man with a resurrected body.

v.5 ruler: now and in the age to come as King of kings (Rev. 19:16).

v.5 loved us: Jesus' leadership can be fully trusted because He voluntarily died for us. He always uses His power to cause love and goodness to increase.

v.7 He is coming: the main theme of Revelation is Jesus' return to earth to rule all the nations (Rev. 11:15; 19:15, 21).

PART 1: John's CALLING to prophesy about the end times

1   The Revelation of Jesus Christ, which God gave Him to show His servants—things which must shortly take place. And He sent and signified it by His angel to His servant John,

2   who bore witness to the word of God, and to the testimony of Jesus Christ, to all things that he saw.
3   Blessed is he who reads and those who hear the words of this prophecy, and keep those things which are written in it; for the time is near.
4   John, to the seven churches which are in Asia: Grace to you and peace from Him who is and who was and who is to come, and from the seven Spirits who are before His throne,
5   and from Jesus Christ, the faithful witness, the firstborn from the dead, and the ruler over the kings of the earth. To Him who loved us and washed us from our sins in His own blood,
6   and has made us kings and priests to His God and Father, to Him be glory and dominion forever and ever. Amen.
7   Behold, He is coming with clouds, and every eye will see Him, even they who pierced Him. And all the tribes of the earth will mourn because of Him. Even so, Amen.
8   "I am the Alpha and the Omega, the Beginning and the End," says the Lord, "who is and who was and who is to come, the Almighty."
9   I, John, both your brother and companion in the tribulation and kingdom and patience of Jesus Christ, was on the island that is called Patmos for the word of God and for the testimony of Jesus Christ.

JUDGMENT   PROMISE   PERSECUTION   PRAYER/WORSHIP

In Revelation 1:11-20, Jesus revealed truths about His majesty and ministry in what He wore, what He said, and what He did. *See article on page 102.*

v.11 Alpha and Omega: the Greek alphabet begins with the letter *alpha* and ends with *omega*. Jesus is A to Z in love, wisdom, and power. He is the sovereign Lord over everything that exists as well as all the events and promises described in Rev. 1-22. He is the First and the Last; see Rev. 2:8. *See note on page 14.*

v.13 Son of Man: Jesus is fully God and fully Man as the pre-existent God and our human High Priest. This title speaks of Jesus as the "ideal man," or one who fulfilled all that God intended man to be, and who leads the Church through history as *Prophet, Priest, and King*. Daniel saw the Son of Man as the one who would come to destroy the Antichrist and rule all the nations (Dan. 7:11-14).
v.13 midst of the lampstands: Jesus manifests His presence in our midst.
v.13 garment down to the feet: this robe signifies that Jesus is our High Priest.

v.14 white: signifying eternity, purity, and wisdom like the Father (Dan. 7:9).
v.14 eyes like fire: signifying that He sees everything, feels fiery desire for us, and imparts that desire to us as He destroys all that hinders love in our lives.

v.15 feet like brass: brass speaks of judgment. Jesus tramples all of His enemies under His feet (Ps. 110:1). He will remove all that resists His leadership.

v.16 holds the stars: stars speak of the messenger-leaders in each church (see v. 20). He tenderly holds and upholds them in His hand.
v.16 sharp two-edged sword: He releases power by His words (Eph. 6:17).
v.16 countenance like the sun: His brightness strengthens and fascinates His people.

v.18 Hades and Death: Jesus has authority over life and death (Mt. 16:19).

v.20 the word *angel* (*angelos* in Greek) literally means messenger. It can be used for a human or angelic messenger. Each letter was written to the main messenger-leader of each church, who is symbolically referred to as a star in His hand.

10   I was in the Spirit on the Lord's Day, and I heard behind me a loud voice, as of a trumpet,

11   saying, "I am the Alpha and the Omega, the First and the Last," and, "What you see, write in a book and send it to the seven churches which are in Asia: to Ephesus, to Smyrna, to Pergamos, to Thyatira, to Sardis, to Philadelphia, and to Laodicea."

12   Then I turned to see the voice that spoke with me. And having turned I saw seven golden lampstands,

13   and in the midst of the seven lampstands One like the Son of Man, clothed with a garment down to the feet and girded about the chest with a golden band.

14   His head and hair were white like wool, as white as snow, and His eyes like a flame of fire;

15   His feet were like fine brass, as if refined in a furnace, and His voice as the sound of many waters;

16   He had in His right hand seven stars, out of His mouth went a sharp two-edged sword, and His countenance was like the sun shining in its strength.

17   And when I saw Him, I fell at His feet as dead. But He laid His right hand on me, saying to me, "Do not be afraid; I am the First and the Last.

18   I am He who lives, and was dead, and behold, I am alive forevermore. Amen. And I have the keys of Hades and of Death.

19   Write the things which you have seen, and the things which are, and the things which will take place after this.

20   The mystery of the seven stars which you saw in My right hand, and the seven golden lampstands: The seven stars are the angels of the seven churches, and the seven lampstands which you saw are the seven churches.

JUDGMENT   PROMISE   PERSECUTION   PRAYER/WORSHIP

PART 2: Revelation 2-3

Jesus gave **SEVEN LETTERS** to seven churches. The instructions Jesus gave to these churches about overcoming sin give us practical insight into what we must overcome today. In these seven letters, Jesus spoke of twenty-two rewards offered to His people to motivate and stabilize them throughout church history and especially in the end-time conflict. *See the article "Overcomers Who Receive Rewards in Revelation 2-3" on page 108.*

REV. 2 **2:1-7 EPHESUS MESSAGE:** a call to return to their first love for Jesus.

v.1 holds: Jesus holds the stars (leaders of the churches) in His hand, signifying that He tenderly helps them (Ps. 16:11; 17:7; 18:35; 20:6; Rev. 1:13, 16-20).

v.2-3 your labor: affirmed for diligent work and for standing for the truth by exposing false teachings (v. 6).

v.4 first love: Jesus corrected them for losing their first love for Him in the midst of their diligent ministry labors. They increased their work but decreased in their love for Jesus. Our work in ministry must flow from love.

v.5 fallen: they had fallen away from the fervent love they once had for Jesus.

v.6 Nicolaitans: the common view among the early church fathers was that they were followers of Nicolas, the Jerusalem deacon (Acts 6:5) who fell into error by distorting the doctrine of grace with his teachings that allowed for low standards of morality. Similar false teachings that distort true "liberty in grace" are increasing in the Church today.

2:8-11 SMYRNA MESSAGE: a persecuted church exhorted to endure.

v.8 First and the Last: this is the title Jesus used most (Rev. 1:11, 17; 2:8; 22:13) for Himself in the book of Revelation. It speaks of His death and resurrection, as Jesus calls us to resist fear in the face of martyrdom. He is the first to be raised from the dead and the first in authority. He has the power to raise us and deliver us from our enemies. He is the first cause and source of all blessing. He created all things (Jn. 1:3; Col. 1:15-19). He has the last word on our life and death. His purpose is the last or highest purpose for our life (also see Isa. 41:4; 44:6; 48:12).

v.9 synagogue of Satan: was made up of Jews in that day who denied Jesus' deity and resurrection, and who persecuted the saints. They also considered His miracles to be the work of Satan (Mt. 12:24; Jn. 8:44).

PART 2: Jesus gave SEVEN LETTERS to seven churches

2 "To the angel of the church of Ephesus write,
'These things says He who holds the seven stars in His right hand, who walks in the midst of the seven golden lampstands:

2   "I know your works, your labor, your patience, and that you cannot bear those who are evil. And you have tested those who say they are apostles and are not, and have found them liars;

3   and you have persevered and have patience, and have labored for My name's sake and have not become weary.

4   Nevertheless I have this against you, that you have left your first love.

5   Remember therefore from where you have fallen; repent and do the first works, or else I will come to you quickly and remove your lampstand from its place—unless you repent.

6   But this you have, that you hate the deeds of the Nicolaitans, which I also hate.

7   "He who has an ear, let him hear what the Spirit says to the churches. To him who overcomes I will give to eat from the tree of life, which is in the midst of the Paradise of God.'"

8   "And to the angel of the church in Smyrna write,
'These things says the First and the Last, who was dead, and came to life:

9   "I know your works, tribulation, and poverty (but you are rich); and I know the blasphemy of those who say they are Jews and are not, but are a synagogue of Satan.

JUDGMENT   PROMISE   PERSECUTION   PRAYER/WORSHIP

v.10 tribulation ten days: some commentators point to the literal ten-day period of the gladiatorial contests in which Christians were thrown to the wild beasts.

v.10 crown of life: the reward of a crown is not synonymous with receiving the gift of eternal life (1 Cor. 9:24-25; 2 Tim. 4:8; 1 Pet. 5:4; Jas. 1:12; Rev. 3:11) and will not automatically be given to every believer. Jesus promised the reward of a crown to those who overcome fear when being persecuted.

v.11 not hurt by the second death: the ungodly persecutors of the saints will be *hurt* at the second death when they are cast into the lake of fire forever (Rev. 20:14). If the saints reject the faith when they are *hurt* by their persecutors, then they will also be *hurt* by the second death. If they overcome now, they will not be *hurt* in God's terrifying hour of final judgment.

2:12-17 PERGAMOS MESSAGE: a call to overcome compromise.

v.14 things against you: Jesus corrected them for allowing false teachings that tolerated immorality. Balaam taught King Balak to seduce Israel into participating in idolatrous feasts that involved immorality (Num. 25). Immorality is all sexual activity outside of marriage (physical, verbal, technological). It grants Satan legal "doors of access" to harm one's life.

False teaching on grace makes people comfortable while continuing in compromise. The true teaching of grace gives us confidence to pursue purity, knowing that it is attainable. It assures us of being forgiven and even enjoyed by God as we resist our sin and continue in the process of spiritual maturity.

v.16 sword of My mouth: refers to Jesus' power being released by His words. He releases His sword of judgment by speaking His word (Rev. 2:12; 19:15, 21).

v.17 manna: manna was hidden in the ark of the covenant in the Holy of Holies (Ex. 16:31-34; Heb. 9:4). This reward speaks of being fed on the deep things of God's Word in this age and in the age to come.

v.17 white: this Greek word can be translated "shining," as of a precious stone.

v.17 new name: speaks of receiving a name or testimony before God of one's faithfulness. God will write this name on the precious stone as a reward.

10   Do not fear any of those things which you are about to suffer. Indeed, the devil is about to throw some of you into prison, that you may be tested, and you will have tribulation ten days. Be faithful until death, and I will give you the crown of life.

11   "He who has an ear, let him hear what the Spirit says to the churches. He who overcomes shall not be hurt by the second death.'"

12   "And to the angel of the church in Pergamos write, 'These things says He who has the sharp two-edged sword:

13   "I know your works, and where you dwell, where Satan's throne is. And you hold fast to My name, and did not deny My faith even in the days in which Antipas was My faithful martyr, who was killed among you, where Satan dwells.

14   But I have a few things against you, because you have there those who hold the doctrine of Balaam, who taught Balak to put a stumbling block before the children of Israel, to eat things sacrificed to idols, and to commit sexual immorality.

15   Thus you also have those who hold the doctrine of the Nicolaitans, which thing I hate.

16   Repent, or else I will come to you quickly and will fight against them with the sword of My mouth.

17   "He who has an ear, let him hear what the Spirit says to the churches. To him who overcomes I will give some of the hidden manna to eat. And I will give him a white stone, and on the stone a new name written which no one knows except him who receives it.'"

JUDGMENT   PROMISE   PERSECUTION   PRAYER/WORSHIP

2:18-29 THYATIRA MESSAGE: the call to no longer tolerate immorality.
v.18 eyes of fire: Jesus' eyes can release judgment and/or impart love (Lk. 24:32; Acts 2:3). He releases either the "fire of grace" or the "fire of judgment" depending on our response to Him.
v.18 feet like brass: brass speaks of judgment. Jesus' feet of bronze speak of His promise and power as a mighty warrior to tread down immorality.

v.20 things against you: Jesus affirmed their love and endurance in persecution, yet corrected them for lacking boldness to confront believers engaged in immorality. Jezebel taught "liberty in grace" with reference to attending idol feasts involving immorality. The *spirit of Jezebel* is that which promotes immorality and idolatry (occult). It is the spirit that operates in those who make, sell, or buy pornography.

v.22 cast into a sickbed: some believers who refuse to repent of immorality are made sick and even die as a result of God's judgment. Satan is permitted to strike them with sickness (1 Cor. 5:1-5; 11:30; 1 Tim. 1:20). This is an expression of His mercy to wake up the saints. If we judge ourselves, then Jesus will not have to wake us up with His judgments (1 Cor. 11:31-32).

v.24 depths of Satan: the deep things of Satan included Jezebel's false teaching on grace that allowed people to embrace immorality.

v.26 power: reward of reigning in the Millennium (Lk. 19:11-27; Rev. 3:21).

v.27 rod of iron: David prophesied that Jesus would dash nations (Ps. 2:8-9) with a rod of iron in the Millennium (Rev. 12:5; 19:15).

v.28 morning star: Jesus is the morning star (Rev. 22:16). The morning star is the brightest star in the sky, seen just before the dawning of a new day. This promise speaks of a deeper revelation of and relationship with Jesus, and a greater understanding of prophetic scriptures (2 Pet. 1:19). Jesus is the star or king from Jacob's family line who was given dominion over the nations (Num. 24:17-19).

18 "And to the angel of the church in Thyatira write,
'These things says the Son of God, who has eyes like a flame
of fire, and His feet like fine brass:
19 "I know your works, love, service, faith, and your
patience; and as for your works, the last are more than the
first.
20 Nevertheless I have a few things against you, because
you allow that woman Jezebel, who calls herself a prophetess,
to teach and seduce My servants to commit sexual immorality
and eat things sacrificed to idols.
21 And I gave her time to repent of her sexual
immorality, and she did not repent.
22 Indeed I will cast her into a sickbed, and those who
commit adultery with her into great tribulation, unless
they repent of their deeds.
23 I will kill her children with death, and all the
churches shall know that I am He who searches the minds
and hearts. And I will give to each one of you according to
your works.
24 "Now to you I say, and to the rest in Thyatira, as many
as do not have this doctrine, who have not known the depths
of Satan, as they say, I will put on you no other burden.
25 But hold fast what you have till I come.
26 And he who overcomes, and keeps My works until the
end, to him I will give power over the nations—
27 'He shall rule them with a rod of iron;
They shall be dashed to pieces like the potter's vessels' -
as I also have received from My Father;
28 and I will give him the morning star.
29 "He who has an ear, let him hear what the Spirit says
to the churches.'"

JUDGMENT   PROMISE   PERSECUTION   PRAYER/WORSHIP

REV. 3 **3:1-6 SARDIS MESSAGE:** a call to overcome spiritual deadness.

v.2 watchful: a lifestyle of prayer with obedience. Watching is the main exhortation that Jesus gave in the context of preparing for victory in the end times (Mt. 24:42-44; 25:13; Mk. 13:33-37; Lk. 21:36; Rev. 3:3; 16:15).

v.3 thief: Jesus coming to us as a thief is an expression indicating that He will come at an unexpected time and in a way that could result in us suffering loss.

v.5 garments: eternal rewards are given for faithfulness (Rev. 3:18; 19:8).

3:7-13 PHILADELPHIA MESSAGE: a call to continue to be faithful.

v.7 key of David: Jesus has the keys of authority over all that God promised concerning the throne of David (Isa. 9:7; Lk. 1:32-33). For example, He has the keys to open doors or positions of authority now and in the Millennium.

v.10 This is the most debated verse about the timing of the rapture.

v.10 I will keep you from: includes a *"spiritual keeping"* that enables the saints to be kept from stumbling in sin in the face of temptation and persecution. It speaks of receiving the grace to not compromise (Lk. 21:34-36; 1 Pet. 1:5).

In John 17:15, Jesus prayed these very words, asking the Father to "keep" believers from Satan. He did not pray that they be taken from the world, but that they would be kept in victory by being enabled to stand strong (Eph. 6:13, 16). This promise includes a *physical keeping* from God's judgment (1 Thes. 1:10; 5:9); sometimes it also includes keeping us from persecution. Not all the saints will be exempt from all physical danger since many will be martyred in the end times (Rev. 6:11; 13:7, 15; 17:6; 18:24; 19:2).

There is a debate that hinges on how we understand the word *from* in the phrase "keep you from the hour of trial." There are two main interpretations: the posttribulation rapture view sees it as being kept from stumbling; the pretribulation rapture view sees it as being kept from the Tribulation period. I respect many who teach the pretribulation view, but I believe it is a significant error.

v.10 the hour of trial: a specific period of persecution of Christians in the first century under the Roman Empire that foreshadows future events.

3 "And to the angel of the church in Sardis write,
'These things says He who has the seven Spirits of God
and the seven stars: "I know your works, that you have a
name that you are alive, but you are dead.
2   Be watchful, and strengthen the things which
remain, that are ready to die, for I have not found your works
perfect before God.
3   Remember therefore how you have received and heard;
hold fast and repent. Therefore if you will not watch, I will
come upon you as a thief, and you will not know what hour
I will come upon you.
4   You have a few names even in Sardis who have not
defiled their garments; and they shall walk with Me in
white, for they are worthy.
5   He who overcomes shall be clothed in white garments,
and I will not blot out his name from the Book of Life; but
I will confess his name before My Father and before His
angels.
6   "He who has an ear, let him hear what the Spirit says
to the churches.'"
7   "And to the angel of the church in Philadelphia write,
'These things says He who is holy, He who is true, "He who
has the key of David, He who opens and no one shuts, and
shuts and no one opens":
8   "I know your works. See, I have set before you an open
door, and no one can shut it; for you have a little strength,
have kept My word, and have not denied My name.
9   Indeed I will make those of the synagogue of Satan,
who say they are Jews and are not, but lie—indeed I will
make them come and worship before your feet, and to
know that I have loved you.
10   Because you have kept My command to persevere, I
also will keep you from the hour of trial which shall come
upon the whole world, to test those who dwell on the earth.

JUDGMENT   PROMISE   PERSECUTION   PRAYER/WORSHIP

v.11 no one may take your crown: Jesus warns them not to allow anyone to influence them to compromise as this would result in the loss of rewards that they could have gained. Eternal rewards can be lost (1 Cor. 3:15; 2 Jn. 8, NIV).

v.12 a pillar in the temple of My God: to be a pillar is a position of honor and authority (Gal. 2:9). Overcomers will have authority in the Millennium.

v.12 I will write on him the name of My God: to have the name of God written on one's heart is to receive greater revelation of His heart and majesty. To receive a new name from God means to receive new aspects of our identity, with new abilities and a new ministry assignment in the age to come.

3:14-22 LAODICEA MESSAGE: a call to overcome lukewarmness.

v.14 Faithful Witness: a faithful witness is one who testifies or says whatever he hears from God without regard for pleasing men.

v.14 Beginning of the creation: Jesus is uncreated like the Father. There was never a time that He did not exist. He is not the beginning in the sense of being the first one created, since He is eternally pre-existent (Jn. 1:15, 18, 30; 3:13; 6:33, 42, 50, 62; 7:29; 8:23, 42; Eph. 1:3-5; 1 Pet. 1:20). He is the beginning of the creation in the sense of being the cause or source of it (Col. 1:18).

v.16 vomit: speaks of Jesus' stomach feeling sick or His being heartsick with concern over them. He is not repulsed by His people who are lukewarm, but feels anguish in His love for them.

v.18 to buy gold: means to acquire godly character which is costly, yet so valuable. This makes us rich in this age by tenderizing our hearts to feel more of God's presence; it also makes us rich with rewards in the age to come (1 Cor. 3:12).

v.18 garments: the reward of eternal garments relates to our acts of faithfulness (Rev. 19:8), and is given in addition to the robe of righteousness that all believers will possess as a free gift (2 Cor. 5:17-21).

v.20 opens: Jesus beckons believers to a new depth in their walk with Him.

v.21 throne: all believers are offered the opportunity to reign with Jesus in the Millennium (Rev. 5:10; 20:4-6). Jesus promised the apostles that they would eat and drink with Him and sit on thrones (Mt. 19:28; Lk. 22:29-30).

11   Behold, I am coming quickly! Hold fast what you have, that no one may take your crown.

12   He who overcomes, I will make him a pillar in the temple of My God, and he shall go out no more. I will write on him the name of My God and the name of the city of My God, the New Jerusalem, which comes down out of heaven from My God. And I will write on him My new name.

13   "He who has an ear, let him hear what the Spirit says to the churches."'

14   "And to the angel of the church of the Laodiceans write, 'These things says the Amen, the Faithful and True Witness, the Beginning of the creation of God:

15   "I know your works, that you are neither cold nor hot. I could wish you were cold or hot.

16   So then, because you are lukewarm, and neither cold nor hot, I will vomit you out of My mouth.

17   Because you say, 'I am rich, have become wealthy, and have need of nothing'—and do not know that you are wretched, miserable, poor, blind, and naked—

18   I counsel you to buy from Me gold refined in the fire, that you may be rich; and white garments, that you may be clothed, that the shame of your nakedness may not be revealed; and anoint your eyes with eye salve, that you may see.

19   As many as I love, I rebuke and chasten. Therefore be zealous and repent.

20   Behold, I stand at the door and knock. If anyone hears My voice and opens the door, I will come in to him and dine with him, and he with Me.

21   To him who overcomes I will grant to sit with Me on My throne, as I also overcame and sat down with My Father on His throne.

22   "He who has an ear, let him hear what the Spirit says to the churches."'"

JUDGMENT   PROMISE   PERSECUTION   PRAYER/WORSHIP

PART 3: Revelation 4-5

Jesus takes the SCROLL: The scroll represents the title deed of the earth and Jesus' battle plan to cleanse the whole earth in preparation for His rule. Jesus' battle plan is seen in the events of Revelation 6-22.

REV. 4 | Revelation 4 gives us a unique revelation of God's beauty in Scripture. We gain insight into God's beauty by meditating on the splendor that surrounds Him.

v.3 God's person: God revealed His appearance in three significant colors (jasper, sardius, and emerald). This gives us insight into how God looks, feels, and acts towards believers. God's glory shines like a *jasper* stone whose light radiates from Him like a diamond (Rev. 21:11). God's heart is like a *sardius* or a deep red gem in His fiery desires for us (Deut. 4:24). Around His throne is an *emerald* rainbow to signify His covenant mercies that cover all the activity of His throne (Gen. 9:13-16). He always acts in mercy. Green is the color of life (plant life).

v.4 God's partners: the elders are enthroned, robed, and crowned. Many agree that these elders are most likely saints (not angels). The honor He gives the elders reveals His desire for partnership with His people as He shares His authority with them. The elders are enthroned with God's authority. Saints will sit on thrones (Rev. 2:28; 3:21; Mt. 19:28; Lk. 22:30). The elders are clothed in white robes, which speak of the pure garments of God's priests. The elders wear gold crowns, as will other saints (Rev. 2:10; 3:11).

v.5 God's power: manifest in lightning, thunder, and voices. Lightning manifests the Spirit's energy and splendor (Rev. 8:5; 11:19; 16:18). Thunderings speak of God's messages sounding forth with power (Rev. 8:5; 10:3-4; 11:19; 16:18). The voices/sounds are probably musical (Rev. 8:5; 11:19; 16:18)

v.5b-7 God's presence: the Spirit's fiery presence is manifest in the lamps, the living creatures, and the sea of glass. *See note on "lamps," Rev. 5:6, on page 26.* The living creatures are seraphim (Isa. 6:1-4). The word *seraphim* means "the burning ones"; they are thought to be the highest-ranking angelic beings. The saints gather on the sea of glass, which is mingled with flaming fire (Rev. 15.2).

v.8 Holy, holy, holy: to be holy means "to be totally separated from" something. God is totally separated from everything sinful; thus, He is pure. God is also separated from everything created; thus, He is transcendent or infinitely superior to everything, because He is "wholly other than" all that exists.

PART 3: Jesus takes the SCROLL

4 After these things I looked, and behold, a door standing open in heaven. And the first voice which I heard was like a trumpet speaking with me, saying, "Come up here, and I will show you things which must take place after this."

2   Immediately I was in the Spirit; and behold, a throne set in heaven, and One sat on the throne.

3   And He who sat there was like a jasper and a sardius stone in appearance; and there was a rainbow around the throne, in appearance like an emerald.

4   Around the throne were twenty-four thrones, and on the thrones I saw twenty-four elders sitting, clothed in white robes; and they had crowns of gold on their heads.

5   And from the throne proceeded lightnings, thunderings, and voices. Seven lamps of fire were burning before the throne, which are the seven Spirits of God.

6   Before the throne there was a sea of glass, like crystal. And in the midst of the throne, and around the throne, were four living creatures full of eyes in front and in back.

7   The first living creature was like a lion, the second living creature like a calf, the third living creature had a face like a man, and the fourth living creature was like a flying eagle.

8   The four living creatures, each having six wings, were full of eyes around and within. And they do not rest day or night, saying:

> "Holy, holy, holy,
> Lord God Almighty,
> Who was and is and is to come!"

9   Whenever the living creatures give glory and honor and thanks to Him who sits on the throne, who lives forever and ever,

JUDGMENT   PROMISE   PERSECUTION   PRAYER/WORSHIP

v.11 worthy: God is worthy of our unqualified trust in His leadership and our sacrificial obedience to His will. To say "He is worthy" means He is worth it.

REV. 5 Revelation 5 gives us insight into Jesus' destiny on the earth as King of kings over all the nations (Ps. 2:8; Dan. 7:13-14; Phil. 2:8-10). Jesus receives the scroll, which represents the title deed of the earth and His plan to cleanse the earth of evil (Rev. 6-19) so that God's glory, justice, and love fill the earth (Hab. 2:14).

v.1 seven seals: the number seven speaks of perfection and completion (Rev. 1:16, 20; 3:1; 5:6; 8:2; 10:3). The seals are not part of the content inside the scroll; therefore, all seven seals must be removed before the contents of the scroll.

v.2 who is worthy: the angel is asking, "Who is deserving and capable to own the whole world and lead all its governments?" Implied in the question is "who has the wisdom, humility, and power to accomplish this?"

v.5 open the seals: to release the judgment events seen in Revelation 6-19. Only Jesus has the ability to open the seals that release God's judgments. Jesus judges sin so that love and justice may increase on earth. God's judgments remove all that hinders love on earth. Jesus' kindness and His judgment are not contradictions, but are two sides of one coin (Rom. 11:22).

v.5 lion and lamb: John sees a Jewish Man who has the fierceness and fearlessness of a lion with the tenderness and humility of a lamb (v. 6).

v.6 seven horns: speak of Jesus possessing all power and authority.

v.6 seven eyes: speak of Jesus possessing all knowledge.

v.6 seven Spirits of God (Rev. 1:4; 3:1; 4:5): speak of the Holy Spirit in His sevenfold perfection with His many diverse manifestations (Isa. 11:2).

v.7 took the scroll: Jesus takes a seven-sealed scroll from the Father. It can be opened after each seal is broken. In taking the scroll, Jesus accepted the responsibility to cleanse and rule the earth.

v.8 bowls full of prayer: Jesus will open the first seal only after the bowls of prayer are full at the end of the age.

10   the twenty-four elders fall down before Him who sits on the throne and worship Him who lives forever and ever, and cast their crowns before the throne, saying:

11   "You are worthy, O Lord,
      To receive glory and honor and power;
      For You created all things,
      And by Your will they exist and were created."

5 And I saw in the right hand of Him who sat on the throne a scroll written inside and on the back, sealed with seven seals.

2   Then I saw a strong angel proclaiming with a loud voice, "Who is worthy to open the scroll and to loose its seals?"

3   And no one in heaven or on the earth or under the earth was able to open the scroll, or to look at it.

4   So I wept much, because no one was found worthy to open and read the scroll, or to look at it.

5   But one of the elders said to me, "Do not weep. Behold, the Lion of the tribe of Judah, the Root of David, has prevailed to open the scroll and to loose its seven seals."

6   And I looked, and behold, in the midst of the throne and of the four living creatures, and in the midst of the elders, stood a Lamb as though it had been slain, having seven horns and seven eyes, which are the seven Spirits of God sent out into all the earth.

7   Then He came and took the scroll out of the right hand of Him who sat on the throne.

8   Now when He had taken the scroll, the four living creatures and the twenty-four elders fell down before the Lamb, each having a harp, and golden bowls full of incense, which are the prayers of the saints.

JUDGMENT   PROMISE   PERSECUTION   PRAYER/WORSHIP

v.9 You are worthy: Jesus is the only One deserving and capable of opening the seal judgments to cleanse the earth and lead all its government in love, wisdom, and righteousness. Jesus deserves this honor because when He had all the glory and power, He laid it down, becoming a man and then dying for us. He did this that we might be able to receive salvation (2 Cor. 8:9). He has proven His love for us over and over by the choices that He has made for our benefit.

Jesus is worthy of our unqualified trust and our sacrificial obedience. The devil is a liar when he says to us, "Jesus is not worth it; He is mistreating you. You might as well just give up and give in because it is too hard and it's not worth it."

v.12-13 Jesus receives an unprecedented measure of glory and favor to rule the earth. First and foremost, He receives this favor from the Father; secondly, the leaders of the earth will lay all their national resources at His feet. Jesus receives in the following seven areas:

- **Power** (political): He receives governmental authority over all nations.
- **Riches** (financial): He receives economic authority over all nations.
- **Wisdom** (intellectual): He has the understanding to restore every sphere of life in the nations during the Millennium (political, economic, family, educational, agricultural, environmental, etc).
- **Strength** (physical): He receives the fruit of all the labor of all the people on earth. The strength of this labor is used for His global purposes.
- **Glory** (spiritual): He receives the authority to impart the power of the Holy Spirit or the glory of God whenever He desires to. For example, He can release it on the kings of the earth during political gatherings, etc.
- **Honor** (relational): He will be the most respected and most listened to man in all the nations. He will also be the most talked about and imitated role model on earth.
- **Blessing** (social): The nations will bless or cooperate with all of His plans and policies. People will fully cooperate with His leadership without resisting Him, resulting in the most unified and joyful work force in history.

9   And they sang a new song, saying:

"You are worthy to take the scroll,
And to open its seals;
For You were slain,
And have redeemed us to God by Your blood
Out of every tribe and tongue and people and nation,
10   And have made us kings and priests to our God;
And we shall reign on the earth."

11   Then I looked, and I heard the voice of many angels around the throne, the living creatures, and the elders; and the number of them was ten thousand times ten thousand, and thousands of thousands,
12   saying with a loud voice:

"Worthy is the Lamb who was slain
To receive power and riches and wisdom,
And strength and honor and glory and blessing!"

13   And every creature which is in heaven and on the earth and under the earth and such as are in the sea, and all that are in them, I heard saying:

"Blessing and honor and glory and power
Be to Him who sits on the throne,
And to the Lamb, forever and ever!"

14   Then the four living creatures said, "Amen!" And the twenty-four elders fell down and worshiped Him who lives forever and ever.

JUDGMENT   PROMISE   PERSECUTION   PRAYER/WORSHIP

PART 4: Revelation 6-22

Jesus' **BATTLE PLAN** is written in the scroll and includes the Great Tribulation judgments against the Babylon religion and the Antichrist's empire. In these chapters, Jesus reveals His main story line of love to cleanse the earth of evil. His battle plan is seen in *five chronological sections* describing judgment events that unfold in sequential order. Each section is followed by an *angelic explanation* that helps us understand why the judgments in that section are necessary and what will happen to God's people.

REV. 6 **THE SEVEN SEALS** are all released by Jesus (Rev. 5:5; 6:1, 3, 5, 7, 9, 12; 8:1).

The focus of the seal judgments is against the harlot Babylon religion for killing the saints (Rev. 17:6). Jesus judges her and those aligned with her by raising the Antichrist up against them. The Babylon religion is destroyed by the Antichrist and the ten kings who serve him (Rev. 17:12, 16). *See the article "The Harlot Babylon: The Antichrist's Two-Stage Strategy" on page 113.*

v.2 first seal: the Antichrist goes forth with political aggression. He is seen riding a white horse to counterfeit Jesus, who rides a white horse (Rev. 19:11).
v.2 arrowless bow: the Antichrist's rule is first gained by a bow without arrows, which is understood to be a threat of war without war breaking out. This speaks of his initial bloodless victories or peaceful conquest.

v.4 given: the word *given* (and/or *granted*) is used twenty-two times in Revelation. God is the unnamed agent giving authority to the Antichrist, the angels, etc.
v.3-4 second seal: fiery red speaks of world war and bloodshed that eventually even causes destruction of the Antichrist's own resources.

v.5-6 third seal: famine and economic crisis which follow war. The black horse speaks of sorrow, sadness, and mourning. The pair of scales in the rider's hand speaks of economics. The economic crisis will result in buying power being reduced to about a tenth of what it is today. A quart of wheat will sell for a denarius (equivalent to one day's wages). Three quarts of barley will sell for a denarius.
v.6 oil and wine: the famine will not touch the ruling class. Luxuries will be enjoyed by a very few who will prosper in this famine. The social inequity between the rich and poor will result in civil strife.

PART 4: Jesus' BATTLE PLAN

Chronological Section #1: The **SEAL JUDGMENTS** against the kingdom of darkness

First Seal: White Horse—Antichrist's Political Aggression

6 Now I saw when the Lamb opened one of the seals; and I heard one of the four living creatures saying with a voice like thunder, "Come and see."

2   And I looked, and behold, a white horse. He who sat on it had a bow; and a crown was given to him, and he went out conquering and to conquer.

Second Seal: Red Horse—Bloodshed and Final World War

3   When He opened the second seal, I heard the second living creature saying, "Come and see."
4   Another horse, fiery red, went out. And it was granted to the one who sat on it to take peace from the earth, and that people should kill one another; and there was given to him a great sword.

Third Seal: Black Horse—Famine and Economic Crisis

5   When He opened the third seal, I heard the third living creature say, "Come and see." So I looked, and behold, a black horse, and he who sat on it had a pair of scales in his hand.
6   And I heard a voice in the midst of the four living creatures saying, "A quart of wheat for a denarius, and three quarts of barley for a denarius; and do not harm the oil and the wine."

JUDGMENT   PROMISE   PERSECUTION   PRAYER/WORSHIP

v.8 fourth seal: death to one-fourth of the earth's people. The pale horse is pale green, which speaks of the color of death and decay (corpse). Death is what happens to the *body*. Hades (or hell) is the place that the *spirit* of an unbeliever goes after they die. The demonic ranks of Hades will run hard behind the spirit of Death to imprison the spirit of unbelievers who die.

v.8 sword: death by human violence will reach unprecedented levels.

v.8 famine: will dramatically increase after the third seal.

v.8 death: the Greek word can also be translated as "pestilence" or "disease."

v.8 wild beasts: an unprecedented number will be demonized since so many demons will be on earth (Rev. 12:9). Many diseases are spread by wild animals. God called these judgments "My four severe judgments" (Ezek. 5:17; 14:21).

v.9 fifth seal: the prayers of the martyrs will release judgment on the Antichrist's empire. By understanding the Spirit's ministry through the intercessors in heaven, we also gain insight into His ministry through the intercessors on earth.

v.10 avenge our blood: shedding of righteous blood of the end-time martyrs will stir Jesus' heart (Rev. 19:2) and strengthen the prayer movement.

v.11 How long: is one of the most recorded prayers in Scripture (Ps. 6:3; 13:1, 2; 74:10; 79:5; 80:4; 89:46; 90:13; 94:3; Dan. 8:13; 12:6-13; Hab. 1:2; Zech. 1:12). This is not a cry for personal revenge but for justice, that God would deliver His people by removing the Antichrist's leaders from their place of influence.

v.11 number completed: there is a limit to the number of martyrs that God will allow before His judgments increase. Murder fills up the guilt of a nation (Mt. 23:31-32), causing its sin to become ripe unto judgment (Gen. 15:13-16). When persecution increases, then the spirit of glory also increases (1 Pet. 4:14).

v.12 earthquake: worldwide geophysical upheaval (Hag. 2:6; Heb. 12:26). Five earthquakes occur in Revelation (Rev. 6:12; 8:5; 11:13, 19; 16:18).

v.13 stars: the Greek word for *stars* used here is *aster* (asteroid). An aster refers to any shining mass in the sky, including asteroids or any flaming debris, etc. Jesus spoke of signs in the sky that point to His return (Lk. 21:11, 25-26, 28).

v.14 moved: every mountain will be moved. Some argue that all the mountains will be destroyed during the sixth seal. This is not possible because the kings, the great men, commanders, etc., hide in the mountains (v. 15-16).

Fourth Seal: Pale Horse—One-fourth of Humanity is Killed

7   When He opened the fourth seal, I heard the voice of the fourth living creature saying, "Come and see."
8   So I looked, and behold, a pale horse. And the name of him who sat on it was Death, and Hades followed with him. And power was given to them over a fourth of the earth, to kill with sword, with hunger, with death, and by the beasts of the earth.

Fifth Seal: Prayer Is Strengthened by Martyrs

9   When He opened the fifth seal, I saw under the altar the souls of those who had been slain for the word of God and for the testimony which they held.
10   And they cried with a loud voice, saying, "How long, O Lord, holy and true, until You judge and avenge our blood on those who dwell on the earth?"
11   Then a white robe was given to each of them; and it was said to them that they should rest a little while longer, until both the number of their fellow servants and their brethren, who would be killed as they were, was completed.

Sixth Seal: Cosmic Disturbances and God's Glory

12   I looked when He opened the sixth seal, and behold, there was a great earthquake; and the sun became black as sackcloth of hair, and the moon became like blood.
13   And the stars of heaven fell to the earth, as a fig tree drops its late figs when it is shaken by a mighty wind.
14   Then the sky receded as a scroll when it is rolled up, and every mountain and island was moved out of its place.

CHRONOLOGICAL SECTION #1

JUDGMENT   PROMISE   PERSECUTION   PRAYER/WORSHIP

v.15 hid themselves: John divides those affected into seven categories of society to emphasize how all segments of society will respond: *kings* (presidents), *great men* (world leaders), *rich men* (financial leaders), *commanders* (military), *mighty men* (civil leaders), *slave* (lower class), and *free man* (working class).

v.16 hide us: people will seek to hide in caves from God's terrifying presence (Isa. 2:10, 19, 21; Hos. 10:8; Lk. 23:30).

v.17 has come: there is debate about whether the Day of His wrath had just begun or is soon to follow. The Greek verb *has come* can look backwards, indicating that the Day had already arrived, or it can look forward to something that will occur. Robert Thomas (*Revelation 1-7: An Exegetical Commentary*, Moody Press, 1992) rightly explains that the Greek verb *elthen* ("has come") is aorist indicative, and refers to *a previous arrival* of God's wrath. It is best to conclude that God's wrath had *previously arrived* beginning with the first seal.
v.17 who is able to stand: Revelation 7 immediately answers this question.

REV. 7 **Angelic Explanation #1** answers the question brought up in Revelation 6:17: *"Who is able to stand in victory?"* John sees 144,000 Jewish believers sealed by God (Rev. 7:1-8), and Gentile believers from every different culture on earth (Rev. 7:9-17) standing strong even in the face of persecution and temptation.

v.2 seal: God will put a seal on His people to protect them from His judgments. God's protective sealing is not limited in the book of Revelation to these Jewish believers. Gentile believers will also be sealed by God (Rev. 9:4 ; Ps. 91, Zeph. 2:3). In Ezekiel's time, God's seal came on all those who were righteous and who cried out against the abominations in the land. God's judgment was not released on Jerusalem until after the angel marked or sealed the foreheads of the righteous (Ezek. 9:4-6). God will seal believers to protect them from judgment as Israel was protected during the plagues of Egypt in Goshen (Ex. 8:22-23; 9:4-6, 10:23) and from the death of their firstborn by receiving a protective mark on their doors (Ex. 12:7-13).
v.4 144,000: these are end-time, Jewish believers, accepting Jesus as their Messiah; they are from the twelve tribes of Israel, as seen in Revelation 14:1-5.

15   And the kings of the earth, the great men, the rich men, the commanders, the mighty men, every slave and every free man, hid themselves in the caves and in the rocks of the mountains,

16   and said to the mountains and rocks, "Fall on us and hide us from the face of Him who sits on the throne and from the wrath of the Lamb!

17   For the great day of His wrath has come, and who is able to stand?"

Angelic Explanation #1: We receive **PROTECTION** from judgments and falling away

ANGELIC EXPLANATION #1

7 After these things I saw four angels standing at the four corners of the earth, holding the four winds of the earth, that the wind should not blow on the earth, on the sea, or on any tree.

2   Then I saw another angel ascending from the east, having the seal of the living God. And he cried with a loud voice to the four angels to whom it was granted to harm the earth and the sea,

3   saying, "Do not harm the earth, the sea, or the trees till we have sealed the servants of our God on their foreheads."

4   And I heard the number of those who were sealed. One hundred and forty-four thousand of all the tribes of the children of Israel were sealed:

5   of the tribe of Judah twelve thousand were sealed; of the tribe of Reuben twelve thousand were sealed; of the tribe of Gad twelve thousand were sealed;

6   of the tribe of Asher twelve thousand were sealed; of the tribe of Naphtali twelve thousand were sealed; of the tribe of Manasseh twelve thousand were sealed;

JUDGMENT   PROMISE   PERSECUTION   PRAYER/WORSHIP

THE SALVATION OF ISRAEL (Romans 11)

In Romans 11, Paul proclaimed three parts of God's plan that all believers must understand to fully cooperate with God's purposes for the Church and Israel.

First, *all Israel will be saved* and brought to fullness (Rom. 11:12, 26).

Second, "blindness in part" has happened to Israel (Rom. 11:25, NIV), in terms of them seeing Jesus as their Messiah, but this spiritual blindness is temporary and will be lifted in the end times. Israel's rejection of Jesus is neither total (Rom. 11:1-10) nor final (Rom. 11:11-32). If we, the Church, are ignorant of this spiritual blindness on Israel, then we will wrongly conclude that God is finished with them.

Third, the fullness of revival on the Gentiles (Rom. 11:25) will *provoke Israel to seek Jesus* (Rom. 11:11) until the fullness of Israel's salvation is manifest (v.12), which will lead to God's glory filling the millennial earth (Rom. 11:15).

7:9-17 John sees Gentile believers from every different culture on earth, with their specific economic and educational pressures, equally enabled to stand strong. They stand in the face of great persecution, temptation, and privation.

v.9 a great multitude: John sees the fulfillment of Jesus' prophecy in Matthew 24:14: "And this gospel of the kingdom will be preached in all the world, as a witness to all the nations, and then the end will come."

v.14 These are the ones who come out of the Great Tribulation: the great harvest seen in v. 9 will come forth during the Great Tribulation. This will be the Church's finest hour. For the last two thousand years the Holy Spirit has been preparing the Church in the nations for this significant hour. The Lord in His kindness will not rapture the Church before her hour of greatest victory.

v.9 palm branches: speak of joy and victory; used in celebrations of the Feast of Tabernacles which is the background to this passage (Deut. 16:13-15).

v.15 serve Him day and night: continual service.

v.15 His temple: there will be no temple in the New Jerusalem (Rev. 21:22) because the whole city will be a worship sanctuary filled with God's manifest presence. God will dwell with His people (Lev. 26:11-12; Ezek. 37:27; Rev. 21:3).

v.17 shepherd: under Jesus' leadership we will be free from the suffering of hunger, thirst, heat, and sorrow that was experienced in the Great Tribulation.

v.17 fountains: we will drink freely from the fountains and river in the New Jerusalem (Rev. 22:1, 17; Jn. 4:14; 7:38-39).

ANGELIC EXPLANATION #1

7   of the tribe of Simeon twelve thousand were sealed;
of the tribe of Levi twelve thousand were sealed;
of the tribe of Issachar twelve thousand were sealed;
8   of the tribe of Zebulun twelve thousand were sealed;
of the tribe of Joseph twelve thousand were sealed;
of the tribe of Benjamin twelve thousand were sealed.
9   After these things I looked, and behold, a great
multitude which no one could number, of all nations,
tribes, peoples, and tongues, standing before the throne
and before the Lamb, clothed with white robes, with palm
branches in their hands,
10   and crying out with a loud voice, saying, "Salvation
belongs to our God who sits on the throne, and to the
Lamb!"
11   All the angels stood around the throne and the elders
and the four living creatures, and fell on their faces before
the throne and worshiped God,
12   saying:

"Amen! Blessing and glory and wisdom,
Thanksgiving and honor and power and might,
Be to our God forever and ever.
Amen."

13   Then one of the elders answered, saying to me, "Who
are these arrayed in white robes, and where did they come
from?"
14   And I said to him, "Sir, you know."
So he said to me, "These are the ones who come out of the
great tribulation, and washed their robes and made them
white in the blood of the Lamb.
15   Therefore they are before the throne of God, and serve
Him day and night in His temple. And He who sits on the
throne will dwell among them.

JUDGMENT   PROMISE   PERSECUTION   PRAYER/WORSHIP

PRAYING FOR JUDGMENT: The saints do **not** pray for judgment to be released before the Tribulation starts. We should be praying for unbelievers to receive mercy and salvation. After the Tribulation begins, it will be a unique time in history, because billions will become **reprobate**, as is seen by their taking the mark of the Beast. A reprobate person one who has no desire at all to repent (Rom. 1:28; Heb. 6:4, 2 Pet. 2:20). After the Tribulation begins, the saints will continue to pray for mercy for the lost, but will add the unique dimension of praying for judgment on the reprobate who will not repent and who will continue to violently oppress and kill the saints (Rev. 19:2). We join the prayers of the martyrs in the fifth seal that the oppression of the reprobate be stopped by the judgment of God.

REV. 8 **The seventh seal:** the strengthening of the prayer movement is in itself a judgment on the Antichrist. Angels offer heavenly incense as directed by the Spirit (v. 3-4) that results in the fire of judgment being cast to the earth (v. 5), and in seven angels preparing to release their trumpet judgments (Rev. 8:6).
Five specific aspects of the seventh seal include: (1) commissioning of seven angels with trumpets; (2) an angel is given heavenly incense to strengthen the prayers of the saints; (3) fire is cast to the earth; (4) cosmic disturbances occur in the sky; and (5) an earthquake occurs on earth.
v.3 another angel: is given much heavenly incense to offer with the prayers of the saints to provide a new measure of supernatural strengthening of the end-time global prayer movement. This angel can only provide this incense as it is given to him by God. Angels and saints will be involved together with incense and prayer that are brought together at the throne (Rev. 5:8).
v.3 all the saints: the prayers of "all" the saints include both the accumulated prayers throughout history that have cried out for His kingdom to come, as well as the increased and intensified prayers offered in the generation in which the Lord returns.
v.4 the angel's hand: the smoke of the incense rises up with the prayers from the angel's hand to be formally presented to God. The angelic involvement in this process signifies that God is pleased with these prayers.
v.5 fire thrown to the earth: in his youth, John wanted to call down fire from heaven (Lk. 9:54-55), in a spirit of pride and ambition. Here, the saints call down fire for the sake of God's glory, just as Elijah did (1 Kgs.18:38).

16 They shall neither hunger anymore nor thirst anymore; the sun shall not strike them, nor any heat;
17 for the Lamb who is in the midst of the throne will shepherd them and lead them to living fountains of waters. And God will wipe away every tear from their eyes."

Chronological Section #2: The **TRUMPET JUDGMENTS** against the Antichrist's empire

Seventh Seal: Prayer Is Strengthened by the Angels

8 When He opened the seventh seal, there was silence in heaven for about half an hour.

2 And I saw the seven angels who stand before God, and to them were given seven trumpets.

3 Then another angel, having a golden censer, came and stood at the altar. He was given much incense, that he should offer it with the prayers of all the saints upon the golden altar which was before the throne.

4 And the smoke of the incense, with the prayers of the saints, ascended before God from the angel's hand.

5 Then the angel took the censer, filled it with fire from the altar, and threw it to the earth. And there were noises, thunderings, lightnings, and an earthquake.

6 So the seven angels who had the seven trumpets prepared themselves to sound.

CHRONOLOGICAL SECTION #2

JUDGMENT   PROMISE   PERSECUTION   PRAYER/WORSHIP

The first four **TRUMPET JUDGMENTS** are supernatural acts of God.

The trumpet judgments have three purposes:
1. **To hinder** the Antichrist's empire by destroying his natural resources.
2. **To warn** unbelievers of increased judgment to come in the seven bowls.
3. **To rally** the saints to gather for prayer (Num. 10:7).

The trumpet and bowl judgments parallel the ten plagues of Egypt (Ex. 7-12).

The trumpet judgments released by the prayer movement recall the plagues of Egypt

TRUMPET		PLAGUES ON EGYPT	
1st: hail with fire	Rev. 8:7	7th: hail with fire	Ex. 9:22-26
3rd: rivers turn to blood	Rev. 8:8-11	1st: Nile turns to blood	Ex. 7:19-25
4th: darkness	Rev. 8:12	9th: darkness	Ex. 10:21-23
5th: demonic locusts	Rev. 9:1-12	8th: natural locusts	Ex. 10:12-20
6th: widespread death	Rev. 9:13-21	10th: widespread death	Ex. 12:29-30

The first four trumpets destroy the natural resources of the Antichrist's empire (Rev. 8:6-12), affecting areas of the *environment* (trees, grass, sea, rivers, sky), *food supply* (vegetation, meat, fish), *sea trade, water supply, light* and *heat* (sun, moon, stars). Their purpose is to destroy resources that support life, yet without directly killing people. The last two trumpets are intensified, in that they directly afflict humans with demonic torment, and result in the death of one-third of the human race (Rev. 9:15, 18).

v.7 first trumpet: a supernatural event like a meteor storm, with hail and fire that burns trees and grass.

v.8-9 second trumpet: a large burning object like a mountain that falls from heaven into the sea, resulting in the destruction of the food supply and sea trade. This sea may be exclusively refer to the Mediterranean Sea.

v.10-11 third trumpet: a meteoric mass causes the fresh water (rivers and springs) to be poisoned.
v.12 fourth trumpet: diminishing light, heat, agriculture, navigation, etc.

CHRONOLOGICAL SECTION #2

First Trumpet: One-third of the Earth's Vegetation Is Burned

7   The first angel sounded: And hail and fire followed, mingled with blood, and they were thrown to the earth. And a third of the trees were burned up, and all green grass was burned up.

Second Trumpet: One-third of the Sea Turns to Blood

8   Then the second angel sounded: And something like a great mountain burning with fire was thrown into the sea, and a third of the sea became blood.
9   And a third of the living creatures in the sea died, and a third of the ships were destroyed.

Third Trumpet: One-third of the Fresh Water Becomes Bitter

10   Then the third angel sounded: And a great star fell from heaven, burning like a torch, and it fell on a third of the rivers and on the springs of water.
11   The name of the star is Wormwood. A third of the waters became wormwood, and many men died from the water, because it was made bitter.

Fourth Trumpet: One-third of the Sun, Moon, and Stars Are Darkened

12   Then the fourth angel sounded: And a third of the sun was struck, a third of the moon, and a third of the stars, so that a third of them were darkened. A third of the day did not shine, and likewise the night.
13   And I looked, and I heard an angel flying through the midst of heaven, saying with a loud voice, "Woe, woe, woe to the inhabitants of the earth, because of the remaining blasts of the trumpet of the three angels who are about to sound!"

JUDGMENT   PROMISE   PERSECUTION   PRAYER/WORSHIP

REV. 9 **FIFTH TRUMPET:** release of demonic army of locusts (Rev. 9:1-12).
Satan has concealed his deep hatred for the human race throughout history, but it will be openly manifest in the fifth and sixth trumpets. "Satan was a murderer from the beginning" (Jn. 8:44). Many will be deluded into thinking that Satan will give them favor for their loyal service to him. He will torment them when God gives him liberty to do so in the fifth and sixth trumpets. God wants them to see the truth about Satan so they can renounce him and be saved.

v.1 bottomless pit: is a temporary prison for fallen angels that will be released during the end times (Rev. 9:1-2, 11; 11:7; 20:1-3). This is a prison for demons bound by chains of darkness; also called *tartarus* in the Greek in 2 Peter 2:4.

v.1 fallen: an angel falls from heaven with the key to open the bottomless pit. There is debate about whether this is a good or evil angel. The argument is focused on the meaning of the word "fallen." Good angels are never described in Scripture as fallen. Therefore, if the angel "fell" in judgment, then this refers to an evil angel (Lk. 10:18; Rev. 12:7-9). If "fallen" means "descended" from heaven, then this is a good angel paralleling the activity of the angel who opens the bottomless pit to bind Satan in Revelation 20:1.

v.4 sealed: the saints will receive a divine seal that protects them from the demonic locusts. God will seal believers to protect them from judgment, as Israel was protected in Goshen (Ex. 8:22-23; 9:4-6, 10:23).

v.5 torment: the anguish of this sting lasting for five months is meant to cause unbelievers to repent, but instead they seek to commit suicide.

v.5 given authority: God is the unnamed agent giving permission (Rev. 9:1, 3, 4, 5). God's authority is seen over these demons in the limits that He puts on their authority: they are not to hurt the grass and trees; they are only to torment men without the seal, and only for five months; they are not to kill them.

v.7-11 the description of demonic locusts: they are compared to horses prepared for battle, wearing golden crowns with human faces. These locusts are supernatural demonic beings, not natural locusts. The details of this prophecy include specific names, rank, description, and torment inflicted. Such specific details in Scripture demand to be interpreted at face value.

v.11 King: Satan's hierarchy includes a demonic king named Abaddon (Hebrew) or Apollyon (Greek), which mean "destroyer"; his name describes his purpose.

Fifth Trumpet: Demonic Locusts that Torment for Five Months

9 Then the fifth angel sounded: And I saw a star fallen from heaven to the earth. To him was given the key to the bottomless pit.

2   And he opened the bottomless pit, and smoke arose out of the pit like the smoke of a great furnace. So the sun and the air were darkened because of the smoke of the pit.

3   Then out of the smoke locusts came upon the earth. And to them was given power, as the scorpions of the earth have power.

4   They were commanded not to harm the grass of the earth, or any green thing, or any tree, but only those men who do not have the seal of God on their foreheads.

5   And they were not given authority to kill them, but to torment them for five months. Their torment was like the torment of a scorpion when it strikes a man.

6   In those days men will seek death and will not find it; they will desire to die, and death will flee from them.

7   The shape of the locusts was like horses prepared for battle. On their heads were crowns of something like gold, and their faces were like the faces of men.

8   They had hair like women's hair, and their teeth were like lions' teeth.

9   And they had breastplates like breastplates of iron, and the sound of their wings was like the sound of chariots with many horses running into battle.

10   They had tails like scorpions, and there were stings in their tails. Their power was to hurt men five months.

11   And they had as king over them the angel of the bottomless pit, whose name in Hebrew is Abaddon, but in Greek he has the name Apollyon.

12   One woe is past. Behold, still two more woes are coming after these things.

JUDGMENT   PROMISE   PERSECUTION   PRAYER/WORSHIP

CHRONOLOGICAL SECTION #2

SIXTH TRUMPET: release of a demonic army of horsemen (Rev. 9:13-21). They will kill one-third of the earth. This is God's mercy to wake up unbelievers who will soon go to eternal hell if they do not repent. Time is running out for them to repent, as the next event is the seventh trumpet and the rapture of the Church.

v.13 golden altar: a voice from the golden altar of intercession commissions the angel to release four demonic angels bound at the Euphrates River. This judgment is connected to the prayer movement, since prayer ascends at the golden altar (Rev. 8:3-5).

v.14 release the four angels: four demonic angels are released to lead a large demonic cavalry commissioned by God to kill one-third of the human race.

v.14 bound: these demonic angels are currently bound (2 Pet. 2:4; Jude 6).

v.14 great river: it is great in size (nearly 1,800 miles) and in significance to God's purposes. It is the eastern boundary of the promised land (Gen. 15:18).

v.15 prepared: these demons are being especially prepared as vessels of judgment in the end times. They have been set aside for a specific work of judgment that involves leading a demonic army of 200 million horsemen.

v.18 a third of mankind: John twice mentions that one-third of the human race will be killed (v.15). Hypothetically, if the world population at that time was 8 billion people, then if one-fourth of the them died (in the fourth seal), this would leave 6 billion people on earth. The sixth trumpet says that an additional one-third of those will die. That would mean another 2 billion deaths. That would bring the death total to about 4 billion deaths in these two judgments. If 4 billion people die in the last three and a half years (1,260 days), then, on average, just over 3 million will die every day—nearly 100 million deaths every month.

v.20 did not repent: though they do not repent at this moment, some will eventually repent (Rev. 11:13). We refer to these as resisters. They are the unsaved survivors of the Tribulation who resist worshiping the Antichrist and do not cooperate with his evil government, though they have no faith in Jesus. Scripture refers to "those who are left" (Isa. 4:3; 10:20; 11:11; 49:6; 65:8; 66:19; Jer. 31:2; Ezek. 20:38-42; 36:36; Amos 9:9-10; Joel 2:32; Zech. 12:14; 13:8; 14:16). Many will be saved and then populate the millennial earth.

v.21 there will be more demonized people on earth than at any time in history, when the earth is dominated by these four primary spiritual strongholds in society: murder, sorcery, immorality, and theft (Rev. 9:20-21).

CHRONOLOGICAL SECTION #2

Sixth Trumpet: Demonic Horsemen that Kill One-third of the Earth

13   Then the sixth angel sounded: And I heard a voice from the four horns of the golden altar which is before God,

14   saying to the sixth angel who had the trumpet, "Release the four angels who are bound at the great river Euphrates."

15   So the four angels, who had been prepared for the hour and day and month and year, were released to kill a third of mankind.

16   Now the number of the army of the horsemen was two hundred million; I heard the number of them.

17   And thus I saw the horses in the vision: those who sat on them had breastplates of fiery red, hyacinth blue, and sulfur yellow; and the heads of the horses were like the heads of lions; and out of their mouths came fire, smoke, and brimstone.

18   By these three plagues a third of mankind was killed by the fire and the smoke and the brimstone which came out of their mouths.

19   For their power is in their mouth and in their tails; for their tails are like serpents, having heads; and with them they do harm.

20   But the rest of mankind, who were not killed by these plagues, did not repent of the works of their hands, that they should not worship demons, and idols of gold, silver, brass, stone, and wood, which can neither see nor hear nor walk.

21   And they did not repent of their murders or their sorceries or their sexual immorality or their thefts.

JUDGMENT   PROMISE   PERSECUTION   PRAYER/WORSHIP

Angelic Explanation #2 answers the dilemma created by Revelation 8-9.

Immediately after the crisis of one-third of the earth dying in the sixth trumpet (Rev. 9:18), there will be great confusion. This will be complicated by the vast amount of deception that has continually come from the many false prophets (Mt. 24:11, 24; 2 Thes. 2:8-9). The human race will be groping for answers.

In Revelation 10-11, an angel explains to John how God will help His people by releasing an unprecedented measure of prophetic insight and direction. The greatest outpouring of the Spirit in history will occur just before the Day of the Lord (Joel 2:28-32; Acts 2:17-21).

REV. 10 In Revelation 10, an angel explains that God has sealed or withheld seven prophetic messages that He will only release in the end times. These significant messages will provide understanding to help God's people walk in faith.

v.1-3 John describes the glory of God on a mighty angel who will release the seven thunders prophetic messages. The implications of the glory on the angel give us insight into how God's glory will be manifest on the end-time Church that will zealously make known the prophetic messages of the seven thunders:

Mighty angel	Operating in the might or power of the Spirit
Robed in a cloud of glory	Experiencing the Shekinah glory of God
Rainbow around his head	Emphasizing God's promises and mercy
Face shines like the sun	A burning heart that results in a bright countenance
Feet are like pillars of fire	Agreeing with God's judgments that remove what hinders love
Feet on the sea and land	Impacting the nations of the earth
Cries out like a roaring lion	Praying and prophesying in the boldness of a lion

v.2 open book: being "open" suggests that the contents of the book are knowable. The angel presumably read its contents to John.

v.3 cried out: when the angel cried out, the seven thunders were released. These will be seven prophetic messages reserved for the end-time Church.

v.4 about to write: John understood the seven prophetic messages enough to be able to write them. An angel told him to seal them up until the end times. The sealing of the book implies that its information is not to be made known. This is similar to Daniel sealing up prophetic information given to him by an angel (Dan. 12:4-10). The two angels are similar in several ways, especially in having a prophetic message for the time just before Jesus' return.

ANGELIC EXPLANATION #2

10 I saw still another mighty angel coming down from heaven, clothed with a cloud. And a rainbow was on his head, his face was like the sun, and his feet like pillars of fire.

2   He had a little book open in his hand. And he set his right foot on the sea and his left foot on the land,

3   and cried with a loud voice, as when a lion roars. When he cried out, seven thunders uttered their voices.

4   Now when the seven thunders uttered their voices, I was about to write; but I heard a voice from heaven saying to me, "Seal up the things which the seven thunders uttered, and do not write them."

5   The angel whom I saw standing on the sea and on the land raised up his hand to heaven

6 and swore by Him who lives forever and ever, who created heaven and the things that are in it, the earth and the things that are in it, and the sea and the things that are in it, that there should be delay no longer,

7   but in the days of the sounding of the seventh angel, when he is about to sound, the mystery of God would be finished, as He declared to His servants the prophets.

8   Then the voice which I heard from heaven spoke to me again and said, "Go, take the little book which is open in the hand of the angel who stands on the sea and on the earth."

9   So I went to the angel and said to him, "Give me the little book." And he said to me, "Take and eat it; and it will make your stomach bitter, but it will be as sweet as honey in your mouth."

JUDGMENT   PROMISE   PERSECUTION   PRAYER/WORSHIP

v.10 eat the book: John "ate" the little book as Ezekiel ate the scroll (Ezek. 2:9-3:3). To eat the book or the scroll means that they spent much time reading the Scripture so as to fully digest its message. Today, forerunners must "eat" or devour the same message that John devoured. In other words, they will devour the book of Revelation to prepare to understand the end-time message.

v.10 sweet and bitter: the scroll tastes sweet because of its message of salvation, victory, and justice for the oppressed. It tastes bitter because of its message of worldwide judgment on the wicked, and persecution of the saints.

v.11 John must prophesy: because God will only release the fullness of His purposes as His people pray and prophesy their release under the leadership of the Holy Spirit.

REV. 11 Revelation 11 tells us that the two most powerful prophets in history will be anointed with signs and wonders (v. 3-6), which will be similar to those of Moses and Elijah and will be a source of great inspiration and direction to God's people worldwide.

v.1 temple: the Jerusalem temple does not exist today. It was destroyed in 70 AD. It will be rebuilt before Jesus returns, and then desecrated by the Antichrist (Dan. 8:13; 9:27; 11:31; 12:11; Mt. 24:15; Mk. 13:14; 2 Thes. 2:4; Rev. 13:12-18).

v.2 tread underfoot: symbolic of being crushed like grapes (Isa. 16:10; 63:2). This speaks of the siege around Jerusalem in the end times by wicked Gentile nations under the Antichrist (Zech. 12:1-3; 13:8; 14:2). Jesus prophesied that Jerusalem would be surrounded by armies in the end times (Lk. 21:20-24). This was partially fulfilled in 70 AD when the Roman armies destroyed Jerusalem.

v.3-6 two witnesses: the two most powerful prophets in history will help the Church by prophesying for 1,260 days, or three and a half years. Their miracles resemble the miracles of Moses and Elijah. They will oppose the Antichrist and proclaim the message of the gospel. Although their actual identities are unknown, some speculate that they are Moses and Elijah, or possibly Moses and Enoch.

v.7 kill them: the Antichrist will kill these two great prophets.

v.8 Sodom and Egypt: Jerusalem is spiritually called Sodom because of the measure of sexual perversion that will occur in her in the end times. She is called Egypt because of the oppression and slavery that many will experience while living in the city of Jerusalem in the end times.

ANGELIC EXPLANATION #2

10   Then I took the little book out of the angel's hand and ate it, and it was as sweet as honey in my mouth. But when I had eaten it, my stomach became bitter.

11   And he said to me, "You must prophesy again about many peoples, nations, tongues, and kings."

11 Then I was given a reed like a measuring rod. And the angel stood, saying, "Rise and measure the temple of God, the altar, and those who worship there.

2   But leave out the court which is outside the temple, and do not measure it, for it has been given to the Gentiles. And they will tread the holy city underfoot for forty-two months.

3   And I will give power to my two witnesses, and they will prophesy one thousand two hundred and sixty days, clothed in sackcloth."

4   These are the two olive trees and the two lampstands standing before the God of the earth.

5   And if anyone wants to harm them, fire proceeds from their mouth and devours their enemies. And if anyone wants to harm them, he must be killed in this manner.

6   These have power to shut heaven, so that no rain falls in the days of their prophecy; and they have power over waters to turn them to blood, and to strike the earth with all plagues, as often as they desire.

7   When they finish their testimony, the beast that ascends out of the bottomless pit will make war against them, overcome them, and kill them.

8   And their dead bodies will lie in the street of the great city which spiritually is called Sodom and Egypt, where also our Lord was crucified.

9   Then those from the peoples, tribes, tongues, and nations will see their dead bodies three-and-a-half days, and not allow their dead bodies to be put into graves.

JUDGMENT   PROMISE   PERSECUTION   PRAYER/WORSHIP

Revelation 11:15, seventh trumpet: the rapture and Jesus' royal procession. The seventh trumpet highlights God's kingdom being released on earth as it is in heaven. He will replace all the governments on earth (Mt. 25:31-32). Heavenly voices declare that Jesus will take over and replace all of the governments on the earth. The seventh trumpet is the last trumpet in the series of seven trumpets numbered by John in Revelation (Rev. 8-9; 11:15). It is the only trumpet which is described as sounding for several days (Rev. 10:7). At the sounding of this trumpet the saints will be raised from the dead and rewarded and the Church will be raptured (1 Cor. 15:51-52; 1 Thes. 4:16-17). The rapture will not be a secret event but will be seen by all people on earth.

Scripture gives three different views of Jesus' second coming. First, Jesus described it according to its cosmic glory (Mt. 24:30-31). Next, Paul described it by its effect on the saints who will all be raptured (1 Cor. 15:51-52; 1 Thes. 4:16-17). Here, John describes its impact on world governments (Rev. 11:15).

Scripture describes three stages of Jesus' royal procession at the time of His return. **Firstly**, Jesus will rapture the Church and travel around the entire earth in the sky on a cloud in a way that" every eye" will see Him. What they see will be so convincing that every unbeliever in "all the tribes of the earth" will mourn (Mt. 24:30-31; Rev. 1:7). This will require a "global procession" over every inhabited place. **Secondly**, on His way to Jerusalem, He will march across the land of ancient Edom (modern-day Jordan) killing His enemies (Ps. 110:5-6; Isa. 63:1-6; Hab. 3:12-13). Their blood will be seen on His robes. **Thirdly**, Jesus will make His triumphal entry into Jerusalem. His feet will stand on the Mount of Olives. He will fight the final battle in natural history and be received as king by all Israel (Zech. 12:1-9; 14:1-5; Mt. 23:39; Rom. 11:26; Rev. 19:11-21). I refer to Jesus' coming as a royal procession because He comes with all the saints (1 Thes. 3:13) and all the angels (Mt. 25:31). *See the article "Jesus' Thirty-Day Royal Procession" on page 116.*

v.15 have become: God's rule is referred to in the proleptic past tense as though it was a finished fact of history (Rev. 12:10). A future event may be referred to in this way when it is certain to occur. It is as good as done.

ANGELIC EXPLANATION #2

10   And those who dwell on the earth will rejoice over them, make merry, and send gifts to one another, because these two prophets tormented those who dwell on the earth.

11   Now after the three-and-a-half days the breath of life from God entered them, and they stood on their feet, and great fear fell on those who saw them.

12   And they heard a loud voice from heaven saying to them, "Come up here." And they ascended to heaven in a cloud, and their enemies saw them.

13   In the same hour there was a great earthquake, and a tenth of the city fell. In the earthquake seven thousand people were killed, and the rest were afraid and gave glory to the God of heaven.

14   The second woe is past. Behold, the third woe is coming quickly.

CHRONOLOGICAL SECTION #3

Chronological Section #3: The **SECOND COMING PROCESSION** and Rapture *(See pages 114-117)*

Seventh Trumpet: The Rapture and the Return of Jesus

15   Then the seventh angel sounded: And there were loud voices in heaven, saying, "The kingdoms of this world have become the kingdoms of our Lord and of His Christ, and He shall reign forever and ever!"

16   And the twenty-four elders who sat before God on their thrones fell on their faces and worshiped God,

JUDGMENT   PROMISE   PERSECUTION   PRAYER/WORSHIP

v.18 four things: four things will occur as a result of the proclamation in v. 15 that Jesus has taken over the governments of the earth. First, the *nations are angry* at Jesus' leadership. Second, the unrighteous *dead are judged*; they are pronounced guilty and sentenced to temporary imprisonment in Hades for 1,000 years until they are thrown in the lake of fire. Third, the *saints are rewarded* when Jesus appears in the sky (Isa. 40:10; 62:11; Mt. 16:27; 2 Tim. 4:1-9; Rev. 19:8; 22:12). Fourth, there is an announcement that the wicked *leaders who destroy the earth are soon to be destroyed* by the bowls of wrath that come next.

REV. 12 **Angelic Explanation #3:** Revelation 12-14 gives us insight into why God's wrath is so severe as to necessitate Jesus destroying and replacing all the evil governments on earth. The reason is that the Antichrist has been violently confronting God's people and His truth by exalting wickedness in the nations (Dan. 8:12, 23-25). Therefore, all his governments must be totally destroyed and replaced. Revelation 12 shows us Satan's rage against Israel and the Church. Revelation 13 describes the Antichrist and False Prophet violently attacking the saints. Revelation 14 promises us that Jesus will dynamically help His people and lead them to victory, and consign followers of the Antichrist to eternal torment.

v.1 a woman: the faithful remnant of Israel through history. The sun, moon, and stars are a reference to Joseph's dream about his parents and their twelve sons (Gen. 37:9-10); they represent Israel's patriarchs and their twelve tribes.

v.2 being with child: the remnant of Israel is pictured as a mother with child; for generations, Israel carried the promises of their coming Messiah.

v.3 red dragon: Satan is the dragon throughout Revelation (Rev. 12:9; 20:2).

v.3 seven heads: represent seven vast empires throughout history that were under Satan's control and who persecuted Israel. They are the empires of Egypt, Assyria, Babylon, Persia, Greece, ancient Rome, and a still-future, revived Roman Empire (Dan. 2:41-42; 7:7, 20, 24; Rev. 12:3; 13:1; 17:3-16).

v.3 ten horns: speak of ten nations in the end times who will work closely together with the Antichrist (Dan. 7:7, 20, 24; Rev. 13:1; 17:3, 7, 12, 16). *For more on the seven main symbols of Revelation, see page 131.*

v.4 his tail: Satan drew, or convinced, one-third of the angels (called stars of heaven) to join his rebellion against God, resulting in them being thrown to the earth in judgment (Isa. 14:12-14; Ezek. 28:12-19).

v.4 devour the child: Satan sought to kill the infant Jesus through the rage of King Herod (Mt. 2:13-21).

CHRONOLOGICAL SECTION #3

17   saying:

"We give You thanks, O Lord God Almighty,
The One who is and who was and who is to come,
Because You have taken Your great power and
    reigned.

18   The nations were angry, and Your wrath has come,
And the time of the dead, that they should be judged,
And that You should reward Your servants the
    prophets and the saints,
And those who fear Your name, small and great,
And should destroy those who destroy the earth."

19   Then the temple of God was opened in heaven, and the ark of His covenant was seen in His temple. And there were lightnings, noises, thunderings, an earthquake, and great hail.

Angelic Explanation #3: The Antichrist's violent **CONFRONTATION** against the saints and all that is good requires that all his evil governments be replaced

ANGELIC EXPLANATION #3

12 Now a great sign appeared in heaven: a woman clothed with the sun, with the moon under her feet, and on her head a garland of twelve stars.

2   Then being with child, she cried out in labor and in pain to give birth.

3   And another sign appeared in heaven: behold, a great, fiery red dragon having seven heads and ten horns, and seven diadems on his heads.

4   His tail drew a third of the stars of heaven and threw them to the earth. And the dragon stood before the woman who was ready to give birth, to devour her Child as soon as it was born.

JUDGMENT   PROMISE   PERSECUTION   PRAYER/WORSHIP

v.5 male Child: is Jesus, who will rule all nations during the millennial kingdom (Rev. 20). He was caught up to God at the time of His resurrection.

v.6 woman fled: in the end times, some of the remnant of Israel will flee from the Antichrist as refugees. God will prepare and care for them. They will have supernatural provision for 1,260 days (three and a half years).

v.7-9 war in heaven: war will break out in heaven between Michael the archangel and Satan in the Great Tribulation. The result is that Satan and all his demons will be cast to the earth. This war will be similar to the spiritual conflict between Michael and the demonic principality of Persia described in Daniel 10:12-21. Some teach that Satan was cast from heaven to earth at the time of Jesus' death and resurrection. However, Paul taught that Satan continues to dwell in heavenly places (Eph. 2:2; 6:12).

v.10 accuser: the word *devil* is derived from the Greek *diabolos* meaning accuser or slanderer.

v.11 overcame: the Church overcomes Satan and the Antichrist (Rev. 15:2). Overcoming is a major theme in Revelation (Rev. 2:7, 11, 17, 26; 3:5, 12, 21).

v.11 blood of the Lamb: our basis of victory is Jesus' finished work on the cross through which He gained victory over Satan and paid our debt, removing Satan's legal right to accuse us (2 Cor. 5:17-21).

v.11 did not love their lives: by pursuing wholehearted obedience to Jesus regardless of what it costs .

v. 11 our testimony: our testimony is what we believe about who Jesus is, what He did on the cross, who we are in Him, and His plan in the end times.

v.12 wrath: causing an increase in demonic torment coming to people on earth.

v.13 persecuted the woman: Satan will be enraged at the woman, or the remnant of Israel, to such a degree that he will seek to destroy the entire nation with a flood of great persecution. Zechariah 12:1-3; 13:8-9; 14:1-5 describes the nations attacking Israel in the end times.

v.14 fly into the wilderness: God will supernaturally provide and protect the remnant of Israel for time, times, and half a time (three and a half years of the Tribulation).

ANGELIC EXPLANATION #3

5   She bore a male Child who was to rule all nations with a rod of iron. And her Child was caught up to God and His throne.

6   Then the woman fled into the wilderness, where she has a place prepared by God, that they should feed her there one thousand two hundred and sixty days.

7   And war broke out in heaven: Michael and his angels fought with the dragon; and the dragon and his angels fought,

8   but they did not prevail, nor was a place found for them in heaven any longer.

9   So the great dragon was cast out, that serpent of old, called the Devil and Satan, who deceives the whole world; he was cast to the earth, and his angels were cast out with him.

10   Then I heard a loud voice saying in heaven, "Now salvation, and strength, and the kingdom of our God, and the power of His Christ have come, for the accuser of our brethren, who accused them before our God day and night, has been cast down.

11   And they overcame him by the blood of the Lamb and by the word of their testimony, and they did not love their lives to the death.

12   Therefore rejoice, O heavens, and you who dwell in them! Woe to the inhabitants of the earth and the sea! For the devil has come down to you, having great wrath, because he knows that he has a short time."

13   Now when the dragon saw that he had been cast to the earth, he persecuted the woman who gave birth to the male Child.

14   But the woman was given two wings of a great eagle, that she might fly into the wilderness to her place, where she is nourished for a time and times and half a time, from the presence of the serpent.

JUDGMENT   PROMISE   PERSECUTION   PRAYER/WORSHIP

v.15 flood: Satan will release a flood of persecution against Israel with the intention of causing her to be swept away or annihilated as a people. The true Church will stand with Israel in this flood of demonic persecution.

v.17 woman's offspring: Satan will war against Gentile believers in Jesus who are spiritual offspring of the woman. He will wage war through his two main weapons, the Antichrist and the False Prophet, described in Revelation 13. In Revelation 13, we see the "counterfeit trinity." Satan counterfeits the Father as he empowers the Antichrist who counterfeits the Son. The Antichrist is supported by the False Prophet who counterfeits the Holy Spirit (Rev. 13:1-2, 11-18). The Antichrist will have a political, military, and economic alliance with ten powerful nations in Europe and the Middle East, making him the richest leader, with the largest empire and the most powerful army of any leader in history.

REV. 13   **v.1 seven heads:** the demonic spirit that inspired seven empires from history that persecuted Israel will operate in the Antichrist's empire. The seven empires are Egypt, Assyria, Babylon, Persia, Greece, ancient Rome, and a still-future, revived Roman Empire (Dan. 2:41-42; 7:7, 20, 24; Rev. 12:3; 13:1; 17:3-16).

v.1 ten horns: speak of ten nations in the end times who will work closely together with the Antichrist (Dan. 7:7, 20, 24; Rev. 13:1; 17:3, 7, 12, 16).

v.2 the dragon: is symbolic of Satan (Rev. 12:3, 4, 7, 9, 13, 16, 17; 13:2, 4; 16:13; 20:2). Satan will give his power and very throne to the Antichrist.

v.2 the beast: the Beast is the name of the Antichrist as an individual and as the name of his empire (Rev. 17:11-13, 17). The Antichrist will think like a *wild beast* without any capacity for mercy. He will be fully human and fully demonized. He will be the most evil criminal in history. His military conquest will be comparable to a *leopard* in swiftness, a *bear* in strength, and a *lion* in fierceness.

v. 3 mortal head wound: a very dramatic event that will launch the Antichrist into world prominence. The Antichrist will seemingly die and then be raised as a counterfeit to Jesus' resurrection. This miracle will occur to the beast as an individual and as an empire. Part of his historic empire referred to as "one of his seven heads" will suffer a fatal wound and then miraculously recover.

v.7 overcome them: the Antichrist will overcome the saints *physically* by killing them (Dan. 7:21, 25; Rev. 6:9-11; 13:7, 15; 19:2). The saints will overcome him *spiritually* by their love for Jesus in the face of martyrdom (Rev. 12:11; 15:2).

ANGELIC EXPLANATION #3

15   So the serpent spewed water out of his mouth like a flood after the woman, that he might cause her to be carried away by the flood.

16   But the earth helped the woman, and the earth opened its mouth and swallowed up the flood which the dragon had spewed out of his mouth.

17   And the dragon was enraged with the woman, and he went to make war with the rest of her offspring, who keep the commandments of God and have the testimony of Jesus Christ.

13 Then I stood on the sand of the sea. And I saw a beast rising up out of the sea, having seven heads and ten horns, and on his horns ten crowns, and on his heads a blasphemous name.

2   Now the beast which I saw was like a leopard, his feet were like the feet of a bear, and his mouth like the mouth of a lion. The dragon gave him his power, his throne, and great authority.

3   And I saw one of his heads as if it had been mortally wounded, and his deadly wound was healed. And all the world marveled and followed the beast.

4   So they worshiped the dragon who gave authority to the beast; and they worshiped the beast, saying, "Who is like the beast? Who is able to make war with him?"

5   And he was given a mouth speaking great things and blasphemies, and he was given authority to continue for forty-two months.

6   Then he opened his mouth in blasphemy against God, to blaspheme His name, His tabernacle, and those who dwell in heaven.

7   It was granted to him to make war with the saints and to overcome them. And authority was given him over every tribe, tongue, and nation.

JUDGMENT   PROMISE   PERSECUTION   PRAYER/WORSHIP

v.8 All on the earth: the Antichrist will have authority and will be worshiped in all nations. This does not mean that he will totally dominate all nations, or that every person will worship him. Some nations will resist him (Dan. 11:40-45). Many unbelievers will resist him until the end. I refer to them as *resisters*. They are the unsaved survivors of the Tribulation who do not worship the Antichrist. Scripture refers to "those who are left" (Isa. 4:3; 10:20; 11:11; 49:6; 65:8; 66:19; Jer. 31:2; Ezek. 20:38-42; 36:36; Amos 9:9-10; Joel 2:32; Zech. 12:14; 13:8; 14:16). Many will be saved and then populate the millennial earth.

v.11 another beast: the False Prophet is called *another beast* only in this verse. Every other time he is referred to as the False Prophet (Rev. 13:11-17; 16:13; 19:20; 20:10). He is the leader of the future worldwide, religious network that will be devoted to causing all the nations to worship the Antichrist.

v.11 like a lamb and dragon: the False Prophet will present his authority (horns) as if he were a gentle harmless lamb, but he will be as much of a cruel beast as the Antichrist. He will speak in a way that seduces the multitudes to embrace the dragon's, or Satan's, agenda.

v.12 worship: the False Prophet will use demonically empowered speeches confirmed by miracles to establish a global worship system for the Antichrist.

v.15 image of the Beast: he will establish a worldwide Antichrist worship system referred to as the *abomination of desolation* (Mt. 24:15; 2 Thes. 2:3-4). It will be based on multitudes worshiping an image (idol or statue) of the Antichrist that will be set up in the Jerusalem temple.

v.15 breathing and speaking: the image will be a demonically empowered statue of the Antichrist that seems to breathe and speak.

v.16 mark: the False Prophet will establish a worldwide economic system to force the nations to worship the Antichrist by taking the mark of the Beast, forcing all to publicly declare whether they will worship or resist the Antichrist. The law will require everyone to worship the Antichrist as God (Rev. 13:12, 15). All who refuse will be considered guilty of a crime against the state and given the death penalty. The image of the Beast and the mark of the Beast will mobilize and finance the Antichrist's global worship movement (Rev. 13:13-18).

v.18 Here is wisdom: God will expose the Antichrist's deception. The Spirit will pour out revelation on all who seek it. Daniel prophesied of messengers who will teach the multitudes of the nations with deep experience and revelation of God's heart, power, and plan (Dan. 11:32-35; 12:10).

ANGELIC EXPLANATION #3

8   All who dwell on the earth will worship him, whose names have not been written in the Book of Life of the Lamb slain from the foundation of the world.

9   If anyone has an ear, let him hear.

10   He who leads into captivity shall go into captivity; he who kills with the sword must be killed with the sword. Here is the patience and the faith of the saints.

11   Then I saw another beast coming up out of the earth, and he had two horns like a lamb and spoke like a dragon.

12   And he exercises all the authority of the first beast in his presence, and causes the earth and those who dwell in it to worship the first beast, whose deadly wound was healed.

13   He performs great signs, so that he even makes fire come down from heaven on the earth in the sight of men.

14   And he deceives those who dwell on the earth by those signs which he was granted to do in the sight of the beast, telling those who dwell on the earth to make an image to the beast who was wounded by the sword and lived.

15   He was granted power to give breath to the image of the beast, that the image of the beast should both speak and cause as many as would not worship the image of the beast to be killed.

16   He causes all, both small and great, rich and poor, free and slave, to receive a mark on their right hand or on their foreheads,

17   and that no one may buy or sell except one who has the mark or the name of the beast, or the number of his name.

18   Here is wisdom. Let him who has understanding calculate the number of the beast, for it is the number of a man: His number is 666.

JUDGMENT   PROMISE   PERSECUTION   PRAYER/WORSHIP

REV. 14 Revelation 14 assures us that Jesus will anoint His people to walk in victory (v. 1-5). Jesus promises to reward His people and to judge the followers of the Antichrist (v. 6-14). There will be serious consequences for unrighteousness. This passage will inspire confidence that righteousness is necessary.

v.1-3 Mount Zion: John saw Jesus standing with 144,000 prophetic singers on Mount Zion in earthly Jerusalem. Most assume that they are the same 144,000 Jewish believers that were sealed in Revelation 7:1-8. Prophetic singing will be used in a significant way by the Spirit to release God's power in the end times (Isa. 42:10-13).

v.4-5 their dedication to Jesus is seen in these five characteristics: *not defiled with women, virgins, following the lamb, no deceit,* and *without fault.*

v.4 defiled with women: this is not a statement about marriage defiling men but about refusing to be defiled by immoral women in relation to the significant increase of immorality and pornography in the end times.

v.4 virgins: they are committed to live as celibates because of their extravagant devotion to Jesus (1 Cor. 7: 29-34).

v.6-13 God will release **four anointed proclamations** to strengthen His people and warn the wicked in the nations.

v.6-7 angels will be involved with the saints in **making the gospel known** with power to all people in the presence of great hostility (Mt. 24:14; Rev. 7:9).

v.8 the anointed proclamation of the certainty of the **total defeat of Babylon** will strengthen the saints and warn the nations.

v.9-11 the anointed proclamation of the certainty of **eternal judgment** coming on all who worship the Antichrist will embolden the saints to steadfastly refuse the mark of the Beast, knowing that all who compromise in this will suffer eternal judgment.

ANGELIC EXPLANATION #3

14 Then I looked, and behold, a Lamb standing on Mount Zion, and with Him one hundred and forty-four thousand, having His Father's name written on their foreheads.

2   And I heard a voice from heaven, like the voice of many waters, and like the voice of loud thunder. And I heard the sound of harpists playing their harps.

3   They sang as it were a new song before the throne, before the four living creatures, and the elders; and no one could learn that song except the hundred and forty-four thousand who were redeemed from the earth.

4   These are the ones who were not defiled with women, for they are virgins. These are the ones who follow the Lamb wherever He goes. These were redeemed from among men, being firstfruits to God and to the Lamb.

5   And in their mouth was found no deceit, for they are without fault before the throne of God.

6   Then I saw another angel flying in the midst of heaven, having the everlasting gospel to preach to those who dwell on the earth—to every nation, tribe, tongue, and people—

7   saying with a loud voice, "Fear God and give glory to Him, for the hour of His judgment has come; and worship Him who made heaven and earth, the sea and springs of water."

8   And another angel followed, saying, "Babylon is fallen, is fallen, that great city, because she has made all nations drink of the wine of the wrath of her fornication."

9   Then a third angel followed them, saying with a loud voice, "If anyone worships the beast and his image, and receives his mark on his forehead or on his hand,

10   he himself shall also drink of the wine of the wrath of God, which is poured out full strength into the cup of His indignation.

JUDGMENT   PROMISE   PERSECUTION   PRAYER/WORSHIP

v.12-13 the anointed proclamation of the certainty of **eternal reward** for being faithful will greatly strengthen the Church.

v.14-20 the anointed proclamation of the certainty of the two end-time harvests: the **harvest of souls** (v. 14-16) and the **harvest of sin** (v. 17-20).

v.14 reaped: the coming **harvest of souls** (v. 14-16) will be the greatest harvest of salvation in history (Mt. 24:14; Rev. 7:9).

v.18 fully ripe: the coming **harvest of sin** (v. 17-20) and its judgment is seen in the graphic terms of Jesus' victory over the Antichrist (Rev. 19:15-21).

v.20 1,600 furlongs: a furlong in the Greek measurement system was about 600 feet. Today a furlong is 660 feet and there are eight furlongs per mile. Thus, 1,600 furlongs is about 200 miles, which is the distance from Megiddo in the north to Jordan (Edom) in the south (Isa. 63:1-6).
v.20 horses' bridles: a horse's bridle is a harness that fits on its head. It is between 5-6 feet from the ground, signifying how deep the blood will be in some places. This will be possible because of torrential rains (Ezek. 38:22) mixed with the blood as it runs through the many valleys in Israel's hilly terrain.

JESUS' ESCHATOLOGICAL WINEPRESS
Jesus will "trample the winepress" around Jerusalem, causing the blood of His enemies to flow for almost 200 miles. He Himself treads the winepress of the fierceness and wrath of Almighty God (Rev. 19:15).

A winepress was associated with the celebration of the harvest. In this case, all of heaven celebrates this glorious harvest of the earth (Rev. 19:1-5).

For the first time in history, all the kings of the earth will be gathered in one geographic area (Joel 3:2, 12; Zeph. 3:8; Zech. 12:2-3; 14:2; Rev. 16:14). After they gather, Jesus will trample the armies of the Antichrist in His winepress (Rev. 19:21). The *wine* that will run into the streets is their blood. Some of it will splash onto Jesus' robe (Isa. 63:1-6; Rev.19:13).

ANGELIC EXPLANATION #3

He shall be tormented with fire and brimstone in the presence of the holy angels and in the presence of the Lamb.

11   And the smoke of their torment ascends forever and ever; and they have no rest day or night, who worship the beast and his image, and whoever receives the mark of his name."

12   Here is the patience of the saints; here are those who keep the commandments of God and the faith of Jesus.

13   Then I heard a voice from heaven saying to me, "Write: 'Blessed are the dead who die in the Lord from now on.'"

"Yes," says the Spirit, "that they may rest from their labors, and their works follow them."

14   Then I looked, and behold, a white cloud, and on the cloud sat One like the Son of Man, having on His head a golden crown, and in His hand a sharp sickle.

15   And another angel came out of the temple, crying with a loud voice to Him who sat on the cloud, "Thrust in Your sickle and reap, for the time has come for You to reap, for the harvest of the earth is ripe."

16   So He who sat on the cloud thrust in His sickle on the earth, and the earth was reaped.

17   Then another angel came out of the temple which is in heaven, he also having a sharp sickle.

18   And another angel came out from the altar, who had power over fire, and he cried with a loud cry to him who had the sharp sickle, saying, "Thrust in your sharp sickle and gather the clusters of the vine of the earth, for her grapes are fully ripe."

19   So the angel thrust his sickle into the earth and gathered the vine of the earth, and threw it into the great winepress of the wrath of God.

20   And the winepress was trampled outside the city, and blood came out of the winepress, up to the horses' bridles, for one thousand six hundred furlongs.

JUDGMENT   PROMISE   PERSECUTION   PRAYER/WORSHIP

REV. 15 John describes a heavenly sanctuary scene in two visions: Firstly, a vision of the victorious end-time saints praising God for His judgments (v. 2-4). Secondly, a vision of seven angels who will release God's full and final judgments (v. 5-8).

v.2 sea of glass: the most recent event that just occurred in the chronological storyline was the sounding of the seventh trumpet to rapture all the saints (Rev. 11:15; 1 Thes. 3:13; 4:14-17). Therefore, every believer throughout history now has a resurrected body. Thus, John is seeing raptured saints with their resurrected bodies standing on the sea of glass, which is before Jesus' throne (Ezek. 1:22, 26). This could be describing the saints in an *amphitheater in the sky*, as a great cloud of witnesses in position to watch and/or be involved in the final judgment events. Jesus marches through Edom (modern-day Jordan), releasing the bowl judgments on His way to make His triumphal entry into Jerusalem to destroy the Antichrist (Isa. 63:1-6; Rev. 19:15-21). At the time of the rapture, the veil between the earthly and heavenly realms will be forever lifted. The fact that John highlights the martyrs here does not limit those involved to martyrs alone. This is similar to Revelation 20:4 when John highlights martyrs who rule with Christ, without limiting the future rule of the saints to martyrs alone.

v. 3 song of Moses and the Lamb: as the song of Moses is the OT song of redemption (Ex. 15; Deut. 32), the song of the Lamb is the NT song. The OT and the NT saints will sing of their experiences of salvation together.

v.3 Great and marvelous: the saints agree with Jesus' end-time leadership and the fruit of His judgments that destroy the Antichrist's kingdom.

v.4 all nations shall worship: the fruit of God's judgments is to cause all the nations to worship Jesus instead of the Antichrist (Ps. 66:1-7; 72:1-4; 86:8-12; Ps. 102:13-22; Isa. 2:3; 49:22-23; 60:14; 66:23-24; Zeph. 2:11; Zech. 14:16-16).

v.5 temple of the tabernacle: John combines the words *tabernacle* and *temple*. The tabernacle in Moses' day was replaced by the temple in Solomon's day. They were the two OT structures in which God manifested His presence, as shadows of the heavenly temple (Heb. 8:1-5; 9:1-10, 23-24).

v.5 testimony: refers to the Ten Commandments, which testify against sin.

v.7 full of wrath: the sin of the nations has come to fullness (Dan. 8:23; Rev. 14:18), so now God's wrath must confront it in full strength.

Chronological section #4: The **BOWL JUDGMENTS** destroy evil infrastructures in society

15 Then I saw another sign in heaven, great and marvelous: seven angels having the seven last plagues, for in them the wrath of God is complete.

2   And I saw something like a sea of glass mingled with fire, and those who have the victory over the beast, over his image and over his mark and over the number of his name, standing on the sea of glass, having harps of God.

3   They sing the song of Moses, the servant of God, and the song of the Lamb, saying:

"Great and marvelous are Your works,
Lord God Almighty!
Just and true are Your ways,
O King of the saints!

4   Who shall not fear You, O Lord, and glorify Your
        name?
For You alone are holy.
For all nations shall come and worship before You,
For Your judgments have been manifested."

5   After these things I looked, and behold, the temple of the tabernacle of the testimony in heaven was opened.

6   And out of the temple came the seven angels having the seven plagues, clothed in pure bright linen, and having their chests girded with golden bands.

7   Then one of the four living creatures gave to the seven angels seven golden bowls full of the wrath of God who lives forever and ever.

8   The temple was filled with smoke from the glory of God and from His power, and no one was able to enter the temple till the seven plagues of the seven angels were completed.

JUDGMENT   PROMISE   PERSECUTION   PRAYER/WORSHIP

REV. 16 The last chronological event to occur before the bowls is the rapture—at the seventh trumpet (Rev. 11:15-19). Thus, the bowls occur **after** the rapture, yet **before** Jesus enters Jerusalem (Rev. 19:11-21). The OT prophets give details about what Jesus will do during His royal procession as He marches through Edom (Jordan) to kill His enemies on His way to Jerusalem (Isa. 63:1-6; Hab. 3:12-13; Ps. 110:5-6; Rev. 19:13). Jesus appears as the "greater Moses" to release the bowls; this is similar to Moses releasing the ten plagues on Egypt (Deut. 18:15-18; Acts 3:22). As the "greater Moses" He will deliver those Israelites who will be held captive in prison camps (Ps. 102:20; Isa. 27:13; 42:7, 22; 49:9, 21, 24-26; 61:1; Jer. 30:3, 8, 10, 17; 31:16, 23; Ezek. 39:23-29; Joel 3:1-2; Amos 9:14; Mic. 4:6; Zeph. 3:19-20; Zech. 9:11-12; 13:8; 14:2; Mt. 25:43; Lk. 21:24.) The trumpet and bowl judgments have many similarities to the ten plagues of Egypt (Ex. 7-12). The bowl judgments are *redemptive* in calling unsaved resisters to refuse to take the mark of the Beast; they are *punitive* in stopping the Antichrist's oppression of Israel. David prophesied that Jesus would dash the nations (Ps. 2:8-9) (destroy the social infrastructures) of the Antichrist's empire (Isa. 11:4; Rev. 2:27; 19:15). Jesus will do this by releasing the bowls of wrath.

v.2 sores: only the Antichrist worshipers receive these tormenting sores.

v.3 like blood: the sea will become like the congealed blood of a dead man.

v.5-7 the heavenly response to God turning the water to blood.

v.5 angel over the waters: power over the waters (sea, rivers, and streams). Different angels have different assignments (Rev. 7:1; 9:11; 14:18; 16:5).

v.5 You are righteous: God's judgments are perfectly loving, wise, and just— never too severe. Men are offended by them. Forerunners will stand as faithful witnesses, unashamedly proclaiming their agreement with His judgments.

v.5 O Lord, the One who is and who was and who is to be: the angel emphasizes God's eternal nature, because only by understanding the big picture of God's eternal plan can we understand the necessity of God's temporal judgments to awaken men to eternal salvation.

v.6 gave them blood to drink: God judges the drinking water to repay those who were accomplices to killing the martyrs. God makes them drink the very thing they thirsted for—blood. God's justice demands that blood be poured out because they poured out the blood of the martyrs (Gen. 9:5-6).

v.7 a voice from the altar: the altar in heaven is the place where the prayers of the saints converge before God (Rev. 8:3-5).

CHRONOLOGICAL SECTION #4

First Bowl: Loathsome Sores on the Antichrist Worshipers

16 Then I heard a loud voice from the temple saying to the seven angels, "Go and pour out the bowls of the wrath of God on the earth."

2   So the first went and poured out his bowl upon the earth, and a foul and loathsome sore came upon the men who had the mark of the beast and those who worshiped his image.

Second Bowl: The Sea Turns to Blood Killing all Sea Life

3   Then the second angel poured out his bowl on the sea, and it became blood as of a dead man; and every living creature in the sea died.

Third Bowl: The Earth's Fresh Water Turns to Blood

4   Then the third angel poured out his bowl on the rivers and springs of water, and they became blood.

5   And I heard the angel of the waters saying:

"You are righteous, O Lord,
The One who is and who was and who is to be,
Because You have judged these things.

6   For they have shed the blood of saints and prophets,
And You have given them blood to drink.
For it is their just due."

7   And I heard another from the altar saying, "Even so, Lord God Almighty, true and righteous are Your judgments."

JUDGMENT   PROMISE   PERSECUTION   PRAYER/WORSHIP

v.8 scorching sun: scorching heat is a supernatural act, not a natural one.

v.9 blasphemed God: they acknowledge God's role in this judgment. They accuse God's character instead of taking responsibility for their sin and repenting (v. 11). As God's judgments increase, the deep-seated hatred of man comes to the surface. Their true hatred for God is now manifest instead of being hidden.

v.10 darkness: in the ninth plague in Egypt, the darkness lasted for three days and it could be "felt" (Ex. 10:21). Demons will be active in this painful darkness so that people will discern, or "feel" it, with great pain in the end times.

v.10 throne of the Beast: this painful darkness will descend on the Antichrist's worldwide centers of government and their infrastructures.

v.12 kings from the east: a coalition of Asian nations, seeing the "confirming miracle" of the drying up of the Euphrates River, will be convinced to finally join the Antichrist's war against Jesus. Up until that time they resolutely resisted the Antichrist's seductions and threats (Dan.11:44).

v.13-14 demon spirits: demons performing miracles will be released by the words of the mouths of Satan, the Antichrist, and the False Prophet. They will deceive the kings of the earth to come to Armageddon to **make war** against Jesus (Rev. 17:14; 19:19). When teaching on the Antichrist and his lying wonders (2 Thes. 2:8-10), Paul prophesied that God would send a **strong delusion** so that those resolved to do evil would go "all the way" in it to such a degree that they would fully embrace what Paul called **the lie** (2 Thes. 2:11). Part of this **great lie** will be in believing that they can make war with Jesus and win. This strong delusion will allow them to act in a way that brings to the surface their deep-seated hatred of Jesus. God will give them over to the full power of their wicked desires (Rom.1:28). Daniel prophesied that in the end times people would progress in great wickedness until it reached its fullness (Dan. 8:23; 12:10; Rev. 22:11).

v.16 Armageddon: Megiddo is a hill in northern Israel. The area around it will be the main military staging area for a three-and-a-half-year military campaign that all the nations finally join just prior to Jesus' return. The word *Armageddon* is from the Greek rendering of the Hebrew name *Har Megiddo*, which means "the hill of Megiddo" (*har* means "hill").

Fourth Bowl: Men Are Scorched with Great Heat by the Sun

8   Then the fourth angel poured out his bowl on the sun, and power was given to him to scorch men with fire.

9   And men were scorched with great heat, and they blasphemed the name of God who has power over these plagues; and they did not repent and give Him glory.

Fifth Bowl: Painful Darkness on the Antichrist's Empire

10   Then the fifth angel poured out his bowl on the throne of the beast, and his kingdom became full of darkness; and they gnawed their tongues because of the pain.

11   They blasphemed the God of heaven because of their pains and their sores, and did not repent of their deeds.

Sixth Bowl: Deceiving the Nations to Come to Armageddon

12   Then the sixth angel poured out his bowl on the great river Euphrates, and its water was dried up, so that the way of the kings from the east might be prepared.

13   And I saw three unclean spirits like frogs coming out of the mouth of the dragon, out of the mouth of the beast, and out of the mouth of the false prophet.

14   For they are spirits of demons, performing signs, which go out to the kings of the earth and of the whole world, to gather them to the battle of that great day of God Almighty.

15   "Behold, I am coming as a thief. Blessed is he who watches, and keeps his garments, lest he walk naked and they see his shame."

16   And they gathered them together to the place called in Hebrew, Armageddon.

CHRONOLOGICAL SECTION #4

JUDGMENT   PROMISE   PERSECUTION   PRAYER/WORSHIP

v.18 great earthquake: this will be the most powerful in history (Isa. 2:19, 21; 13:13; Ezek. 38:19; Hag. 2:6, 21; Zech. 14:4-5; Heb. 12:26-27). Jerusalem will be divided into three parts, and Babylon and the cities of the earth will fall.
v.19 great city: Jerusalem is the great city referred to here (Rev. 11:8). Babylon is also called the great city (Rev. 14:8; 17:18; 18:10, 16, 18, 19, 21).
v.20 islands/mountains: flee from sight by being covered by the ocean.
v.21 great hail: a talent is approximately 100 pounds. Hail was the seventh plague of Egypt (Ex. 9:18-35). Moses' law required that idol worshipers be stoned to death (Lev. 24:16; Deut. 17:2-5). The Antichrist's worship movement will be idolatrous. Jesus will stone them to death from heaven with large hailstones.

REV. 17 **Angelic Explanation #4** Revelation 17:1-19:10 reveals how deeply Babylon's seduction will infiltrate all levels of society and explains why the bowls of wrath are necessary. David prophesied that the Messiah would dash the nations to pieces in the end times (Ps. 2:9; Rev. 2:27). Jesus will do this by releasing the seven bowls, thereby utterly destroying all infrastructures of society that have been influenced by the seductions of Babylon.

Revelation 17-18 is one of the most significant end-time prophecies because it gives us insight into Satan's strategy to deceive the nations. The harlot Babylon will primarily be a religious (Rev. 17) and economic (Rev. 18) network. Revelation 17 focuses on Babylon's religion as a harlot with seductive power, engaging in cruel persecution. This harlot is the counterfeit to the Bride of Christ and will be a counterfeit justice movement, unifying multitudes from many different religions. Revelation 17 looks back to the time when Babylon functions as a worldwide religion in the time before the Tribulation.
v.1 sits on the water: the fact that the harlot sits on many waters means she will have authority over many nations (v.,15). She will seduce and control the world's most powerful leaders (kings and merchants).
v.2 made drunk: the harlot's system will cause the nations to be drunk with her seductions. These seductions include great benefits such as humanitarian aid, unified religion (that minimizes wars) and a prosperous world economy. The nations will get drunk or intoxicated with her promises of goodness, prosperity, compassion, and theology of tolerance based on deception. *See page 113.*

CHRONOLOGICAL SECTION #4

Seventh Bowl: Earthquake, Hail, and the Final Fall of Babylon

17 Then the seventh angel poured out his bowl into the air, and a loud voice came out of the temple of heaven, from the throne, saying, "It is done!"

18 And there were noises and thunderings and lightnings; and there was a great earthquake, such a mighty and great earthquake as had not occurred since men were on the earth.

19 Now the great city was divided into three parts, and the cities of the nations fell. And great Babylon was remembered before God, to give her the cup of the wine of the fierceness of His wrath.

20 Then every island fled away, and the mountains were not found.

21 And great hail from heaven fell upon men, each hailstone about the weight of a talent. Men blasphemed God because of the plague of the hail, since that plague was exceedingly great.

ANGELIC EXPLANATION #4

Angelic Explanation #4: The **SEDUCTION** of Babylon's evil religion infiltrates all the structures of society, requiring that Babylon be totally destroyed

17 Then one of the seven angels who had the seven bowls came and talked with me, saying to me, "Come, I will show you the judgment of the great harlot who sits on many waters,

2 with whom the kings of the earth committed fornication, and the inhabitants of the earth were made drunk with the wine of her fornication."

3 So he carried me away in the Spirit into the wilderness. And I saw a woman sitting on a scarlet beast which was full of names of blasphemy, having seven heads and ten horns.

JUDGMENT   PROMISE   PERSECUTION   PRAYER/WORSHIP

v.4 arrayed in purple: the harlot religion will have great prominence; being arrayed in purple signifies her royal status.

v.4 adorned with gold: the harlot religion will be the wealthiest religious network in history. The elite financial leaders of the earth will give their allegiance to her.

v.4 golden cup: she will "serve" the nations with her cup, which will appear golden (valuable and good). She will offer unprecedented humanitarian service in helping the poor of the earth.

v.4 abomination: her cup, in reality, will be full of abomination and filth. Abomination refers to idolatrous and demonic activity. In the Old Testament, abominations refer to idolatry. Filthiness points to her moral perversions.

v.5 Mystery Babylon: the harlot's name was a mystery. John was surprised that she was the mother of harlots, or the source of false religion through history. Her mysterious name is linked to her origin at the tower of Babel (where Babylon began). Babel was the city in which the first organized religion developed, resulting in the first organized rebellion against God (Gen. 11).

v.6 drunk with blood: the harlot will have a murderous heart despite her humanitarian appearance. Babylon will kill the saints because of their love for Jesus and for being faithful witnesses against her abominations. The influence of the harlot will cause multitudes to be drunk, or intoxicated, with the blood of the saints who expose her. The more she kills, the bolder she will become in killing the saints. She will hate everyone who is loyal to Jesus. The greatest threat to this harlot religion will be the prayers of the saints.

v.7 heads and horns: the seven heads represent seven vast empires that were under the Antichrist's control and who persecuted Israel. They are Egypt, Assyria, Babylon, Persia, Greece, ancient Rome and a still-future, revived Roman Empire (Dan. 2:41-42; 7:7, 20, 24; Rev. 12:3; 13:1; 17:3-16).

v.12 ten horns: speak of a future ten-nation confederation of ten kings who will each enthusiastically come under the Antichrist's authority (Dan. 2:39-42; 7:7, 20, 24; 11:36-45; Rev. 12:3; 13:1; 17:3, 7, 12, 16).

v.13 give their authority: the ten nations will obey the Antichrist and submit their resources to him.

ANGELIC EXPLANATION #4

4   The woman was arrayed in purple and scarlet, and adorned with gold and precious stones and pearls, having in her hand a golden cup full of abominations and the filthiness of her fornication.

5   And on her forehead a name was written:

MYSTERY, BABYLON THE GREAT, THE MOTHER OF HARLOTS AND OF THE ABOMINATIONS OF THE EARTH.

6   I saw the woman, drunk with the blood of the saints and with the blood of the martyrs of Jesus. And when I saw her, I marveled with great amazement.

7   But the angel said to me, "Why did you marvel? I will tell you the mystery of the woman and of the beast that carries her, which has the seven heads and the ten horns.

8   The beast that you saw was, and is not, and will ascend out of the bottomless pit and go to perdition. And those who dwell on the earth will marvel, whose names are not written in the Book of Life from the foundation of the world, when they see the beast that was, and is not, and yet is.

9   "Here is the mind which has wisdom: The seven heads are seven mountains on which the woman sits.

10   There are also seven kings. Five have fallen, one is, and the other has not yet come. And when he comes, he must continue a short time.

11   The beast that was, and is not, is himself also the eighth, and is of the seven, and is going to perdition.

12   The ten horns which you saw are ten kings who have received no kingdom as yet, but they receive authority for one hour as kings with the beast.

13   These are of one mind, and they will give their power and authority to the beast.

JUDGMENT   PROMISE   PERSECUTION   PRAYER/WORSHIP

v.14 make war: they will go to war against Jesus (Rev. 19:17-21).

v.16 hate the harlot: surprisingly, the harlot religion will be hated and destroyed by the jealousy of the ten primary kings who serve the Antichrist. They will burn the harlot at the beginning of the Great Tribulation so that the Antichrist can replace the harlot's "voluntary religion" of tolerance with his own "mandatory religion" that will be forced on everyone with the threat of death (Rev. 13:14-17).

Satan's purpose for the tolerant harlot religion is as a "forerunner" to break down the conscience of the nations to prepare them for a far more evil religion that worships Satan and the Antichrist.

v.17 God put it in their hearts: God has a significant purpose for allowing the Antichrist to rally such a large resource base that will involve the political, military, and financial strengths of these ten strong nations. Before Jesus returns to rule all the nations in righteousness, God will allow Satan to make his "best offer" to call the nations to follow him and his ways of evil. God wants the nations to choose between Jesus and Satan, and holiness and wickedness.

REV. 18 **God will judge the harlot Babylon in two stages**

The first stage of judgment is on the religious network and occurs at the beginning of the Great Tribulation at the hands of the ten kings (Rev. 17:16).

The second stage of God's judgment is on the economic network at the end of the Great Tribulation (Rev. 18:8). *See page 113 for more on these two stages.*

v.2 Babylon: the end-time city of Babylon will be the literal, rebuilt, ancient city of Babylon in Iraq (fifty miles south of Baghdad). It will function as the economic center for the Antichrist. It will seduce many to sin and will persecute the saints (Rev. 17:6; 18:24; 19:2). As Jerusalem suddenly came out of the ashes and was rebuilt, so Babylon will be suddenly rebuilt. The prophets declared that Babylon will be suddenly and permanently destroyed (Isa: 13-14; Jer. 50-51). These prophecies have not yet been completely fulfilled.

v.5 reached to heaven: sin will be allowed to reach its fullness in the end times. The harlot Babylon is the context in which the nations will reach the heights of sin and their experience of the demonic realm (Dan. 8:23).

ANGELIC EXPLANATION #4

14   These will make war with the Lamb, and the Lamb will overcome them, for He is Lord of lords and King of kings; and those who are with Him are called, chosen, and faithful."

15   Then he said to me, "The waters which you saw, where the harlot sits, are peoples, multitudes, nations, and tongues.

16   And the ten horns which you saw on the beast, these will hate the harlot, make her desolate and naked, eat her flesh and burn her with fire.

17   For God has put it into their hearts to fulfill His purpose, to be of one mind, and to give their kingdom to the beast, until the words of God are fulfilled.

18   And the woman whom you saw is that great city which reigns over the kings of the earth."

18 After these things I saw another angel coming down from heaven, having great authority, and the earth was illuminated with his glory.

2   And he cried mightily with a loud voice, saying, "Babylon the great is fallen, is fallen, and has become a dwelling place of demons, a prison for every foul spirit, and a cage for every unclean and hated bird!

3   For all the nations have drunk of the wine of the wrath of her fornication, the kings of the earth have committed fornication with her, and the merchants of the earth have become rich through the abundance of her luxury."

4   And I heard another voice from heaven saying, "Come out of her, my people, lest you share in her sins, and lest you receive of her plagues.

5   For her sins have reached to heaven, and God has remembered her iniquities.

6   Render to her just as she rendered to you, and repay her double according to her works; in the cup which she has mixed, mix double for her.

JUDGMENT   PROMISE   PERSECUTION   PRAYER/WORSHIP

v.7 I sit as queen: Babylon will be filled with pride and false optimism. She will say in her heart that she sits, or rules over the nations, with the royal status of a queen with great strength and dignity. Her false optimism is seen in refusing to believe that God's judgment could ever destroy her.

v.8 her plagues: a four-fold judgment from God of death, mourning, famine, and fire will come suddenly and unexpectedly. As the Church boldly prophesies Babylon's destruction, she will be provoked to great anger.

v.9 weep and lament: the royal families of the earth will mourn over her sudden destruction because her economic crisis will greatly affect them.

v.10 at a distance: they distance themselves from her crisis (v. 15, 17).

v.11, 15 merchants weep: they mourn their great financial loss (Rev. 18:3, 11, 15, 23) and stand in strong disagreement with God's judgment on her.

v.12-13 Eight main groups of merchandise:
- Precious metals and stones (gold, silver, precious stones, pearls)
- Clothing (fine linen, purple, silk, scarlet)
- Building materials (citron wood, ivory, precious wood, bronze, iron, marble)
- Spices (cinnamon, incense, fragrant oil, frankincense)
- Foods (wine, oil, flour, wheat)
- Animals (cattle, sheep, horses)
- Transportation (chariots, used in war)
- Human (human trafficking/slavery, bodies and souls of men)

v.16 great city: Babylon is called the great city (Rev. 14:8; 16:19; 17:18; 18:10, 16, 18, 19, 21). Jerusalem is also called the great city (Rev. 11:8; 16:19).

Babylon will be adorned with gold to show her royal status (Rev. 17:4; 18:16).

v.17 shipping industry: includes shipmasters, sailors, sea traders (v. 19).

v.17 in one hour: her fall will not be gradual, but will come suddenly and unexpectedly (v. 10,19). This distinguishes her judgment from ancient Babylon's.

v.18 burned: Babylon will be burned with fire (Rev. 17:16; 18:8-9, 18),

v.19 became desolate: means to be rendered unfit for habitation and to be devoid of inhabitants (Rev. 17:16; 18:19). This is in great contrast to her once-thriving streets filled with people.

ANGELIC EXPLANATION #4

7   In the measure that she glorified herself and lived luxuriously, in the same measure give her torment and sorrow; for she says in her heart, 'I sit as queen, and am no widow, and will not see sorrow.'

8   Therefore her plagues will come in one day—death and mourning and famine. And she will be utterly burned with fire, for strong is the Lord God who judges her.

9   The kings of the earth who committed fornication and lived luxuriously with her will weep and lament for her, when they see the smoke of her burning,

10   standing at a distance for fear of her torment, saying, 'Alas, alas, that great city Babylon, that mighty city! For in one hour your judgment has come.'

11   And the merchants of the earth will weep and mourn over her, for no one buys their merchandise anymore:

12   merchandise of gold and silver, precious stones and pearls, fine linen and purple, silk and scarlet, every kind of citron wood, every kind of object of ivory, every kind of object of most precious wood, bronze, iron, and marble;

13   and cinnamon and incense, fragrant oil and frankincense, wine and oil, fine flour and wheat, cattle and sheep, horses and chariots, and bodies and souls of men.

14   The fruit that your soul longed for has gone from you, and all the things which are rich and splendid have gone from you, and you shall find them no more at all.

15   The merchants of these things, who became rich by her, will stand at a distance for fear of her torment, weeping and wailing,

16   and saying, 'Alas, alas, that great city that was clothed in fine linen, purple, and scarlet, and adorned with gold and precious stones and pearls!

17   For in one hour such great riches came to nothing.' Every shipmaster, all who travel by ship, sailors, and as many as trade on the sea, stood at a distance

JUDGMENT   PROMISE   PERSECUTION   PRAYER/WORSHIP

v.19 became rich: her wealth comes from international trade as indicated by the prominence of ships (Rev. 18:17, 19). John emphasized luxury, mentioning it three times (Rev. 18:3, 7, 9); the rich are highlighted four times (Rev. 18:3, 14, 15, 19), and merchants four times (Rev. 18:3, 11, 15, 23). The kings or political leaders will support her agenda in order to gain her wealth.

v.20 Rejoice over her: God called all to rejoice over her judgment, not to mourn it or pray against it. All in heaven agree with Jesus' judgment on Babylon (Rev. 19:1-4). God takes full responsibility for the decision to totally destroy her with judgment (Jer. 51:53-56; Rev. 18:8).

v.20 apostles and prophets: will be on earth and functioning in the end-time Church (Acts 2:17; Eph. 4:13; Rev. 11:10; 16:6; 18:20; 18:24).

v.21 with violence: Babylon will be judged with great violence because she was so violent.

v.22 anymore: the city will be so totally destroyed that the normal elements in society, such as musicians, craftsmen, stoneworkers, shining lamps and even wedding ceremonies, will no longer exist.

v.23 by your sorcery: Babylon will deceive the nations by occult practices called sorcery, which is a combination of drugs and demonic power (witchcraft). Her dark supernatural power will fascinate people and appear to be good.

v.24 blood of prophets and saints: Babylon will murder the prophets for speaking out, and murder the saints in general for publicly standing with the prophets (Rev. 17:6; 18:24; 19:2).

REV. 19 **v.1 great multitude:** those in heaven praise God for judging Babylon in fulfillment of Revelation 18:20. This is in great contrast to the angry attitude of the unbelievers on earth to God's judgment on her.

v.1 Alleluia: God is praised with great enthusiasm, as seen in the four uses of the word *alleluia* (19:1, 3, 4, 6). This is the only time the word *alleluia* is mentioned in the New Testament. *Alleluia* is Hebrew for "praise the Lord." In the OT, *alleluia* is usually used in the context of God's judgment on His enemies.

v.2 judged the harlot: immorality and bloodshed are the two main reasons that she received such severe judgment (Rev. 19:21; 17:4; 18:3, 9; 19:2).

ANGELIC EXPLANATION #4

18   and cried out when they saw the smoke of her burning, saying, 'What is like this great city?'

19   They threw dust on their heads and cried out, weeping and wailing, and saying, 'Alas, alas, that great city, in which all who had ships on the sea became rich by her wealth! For in one hour she is made desolate.'

20   Rejoice over her, O heaven, and you holy apostles and prophets, for God has avenged you on her!"

21   Then a mighty angel took up a stone like a great millstone and threw it into the sea, saying, "Thus with violence the great city Babylon shall be thrown down, and shall not be found anymore.

22   The sound of harpists, musicians, flutists, and trumpeters shall not be heard in you anymore. No craftsman of any craft shall be found in you anymore, and the sound of a millstone shall not be heard in you anymore.

23   The light of a lamp shall not shine in you anymore, and the voice of bridegroom and bride shall not be heard in you anymore. For your merchants were the great men of the earth, for by your sorcery all the nations were deceived.

24   And in her was found the blood of prophets and saints, and of all who were slain on the earth."

19   After these things I heard a loud voice of a great multitude in heaven, saying, "Alleluia! Salvation and glory and honor and power belong to the Lord our God!

2   For true and righteous are His judgments, because He has judged the great harlot who corrupted the earth with her fornication; and He has avenged on her the blood of His servants shed by her."

JUDGMENT   PROMISE   PERSECUTION   PRAYER/WORSHIP

v.3 forever and ever: they agree with God's judgments lasting forever.

v.7 made ready: the end-time Church will make herself ready in the grace of God. When Jesus returns, the Church worldwide will be spotless and without any compromise (Eph. 5:27). The maturing of the Church worldwide will be one of the most significant fruits of the Great Tribulation.

v.7 marriage supper of the Lamb: their marriage will be celebrated with a supper. The marriage supper may continue for the entire 1,000 years of the Millennium. Jesus is the Bridegroom God. He is betrothed or engaged to His Bride in this age (2 Cor. 11:2-3). The marriage will be "consummated" at the time of Jesus' return. His Bride is the redeemed from all history. The revelation of the Bridegroom God is seen through history (Isa. 54:6; 62:5; Jer. 2:2; 31:32; Ezek. 16:7-14; Hos. 2:14-21; Mt. 9:14-16; Jn. 3:29; 2 Cor. 11:2; Eph. 5:25-32; Rev. 19:7-9; 21:2, 9; 22:17; wedding parables: Mt. 22:2-14; 25:1-13).

v.8 arrayed in linen: part of the saints' reward will be expressed in the clothing they receive, which expresses their love and obedience for Jesus in this age. Their rewards were given to them at the seventh trumpet (Rev. 11:18).

v.10 spirit of prophecy: the essence of true prophecy is to reveal what is near and dear to Jesus' heart, as confirmed in Scripture.

Jesus' TRIUMPHAL ENTRY into Jerusalem is the high point of history. Jesus is seen as He approaches Jerusalem on a white horse. Jesus will return in the context of a military conflict centered around Jerusalem (Joel 3:2, 12; Zech. 12:3; 14:2; Zeph. 3:8). He will march into Jerusalem as a Warrior-King (Rev. 19:11-21) during history's greatest military conflict to deliver Israel and be received by Israel as their king (Zech. 14:4; Mt. 23:39).

The seventh bowl is the last event to occur in the chronological story line (Rev. 16:17-21), in which Jesus will march in His royal procession through Edom (Jordan) to kill His enemies on His way to Jerusalem (Isa. 63:1-6; Hab. 3:12-13; Ps. 110:5-6; Rev. 19:13). When He arrives in Jerusalem, He will destroy all the kings and their armies who followed the Antichrist (Rev. 19:19-21). Then Jesus will replace all the governments on earth with righteous leaders (Mt. 25:32).

ANGELIC EXPLANATION #4

3   Again they said, "Alleluia! Her smoke rises up forever and ever!"

4   And the twenty-four elders and the four living creatures fell down and worshiped God who sat on the throne, saying, "Amen! Alleluia!"

5   Then a voice came from the throne, saying, "Praise our God, all you His servants and those who fear Him, both small and great!"

6   And I heard, as it were, the voice of a great multitude, as the sound of many waters and as the sound of mighty thunderings, saying, "Alleluia! For the Lord God Omnipotent reigns!

7   Let us be glad and rejoice and give Him glory, for the marriage of the Lamb has come, and His wife has made herself ready."

8   And to her it was granted to be arrayed in fine linen, clean and bright, for the fine linen is the righteous acts of the saints.

9   Then he said to me, "Write: 'Blessed are those who are called to the marriage supper of the Lamb!'" And he said to me, "These are the true sayings of God."

10   And I fell at his feet to worship him. But he said to me, "See that you do not do that! I am your fellow servant, and of your brethren who have the testimony of Jesus. Worship God! For the testimony of Jesus is the spirit of prophecy."

Chronological Section #5: Jesus' **TRIUMPHAL ENTRY** into Jerusalem

11   Now I saw heaven opened, and behold, a white horse. And He who sat on him was called Faithful and True, and in righteousness He judges and makes war.

12   His eyes were like a flame of fire, and on His head were many crowns. He had a name written that no one knew except Himself.

JUDGMENT   PROMISE   PERSECUTION   PRAYER/WORSHIP

v.13 robe dipped in blood: the word *dipped* comes from the Greek word *baptō* (baptize), which means *sprinkled* or *soaked*. The blood on Jesus' robe is from His enemies, whom He will kill while marching through Edom (modern-day Jordan) on His way to Jerusalem (Ps. 110:5-6; Isa. 34:5-10; 63:1-6; Hab. 3:12-13). For blood to get on His robe means that He will be involved in close combat. This will make a public statement that the bloody conflict was absolutely necessary. The robe of the high priest was a long outer garment.

v.14 armies followed Him: the saints will be with Jesus when He battles against the Antichrist (Zech. 14:5; 1 Thes. 4:14). Some of the several billion of the redeemed from all history will be with Jesus *on the ground* riding white horses. Do some of the redeemed witness the events from the air?

v.15 out of His mouth goes a sword: by the very words of His mouth Jesus commands that His judgments, as well as the swords of His army, be released.

v.15 strike the nations: Jesus will break the government and infrastructure of nations with His sword and rod (Isa.11:4; Ps. 2:9).

v.15 treads the winepress of wrath: the blood of His enemies will flow for almost 200 miles. *See the notes on Revelation 14:20 on page 62.*

v.17-18 all the birds gather: the flesh-eating birds of the earth will gather to eat the flesh of untold millions in the Antichrist's army who will be killed (Isa. 18:6; Ezek. 39:4; Mt. 24:28; Lk. 17:37). This is referred to as God's sacrificial meal for the birds (Ezek. 39:17-20). The numbers who die will be so great that it will take seven months to bury them (Ezek. 39:11-16).

v.19 make war against Jesus: the Antichrist and his army will declare war on Jesus (Rev. 17:14). Satan will deceive the kings into coming to Armageddon for this great battle (Rev. 16:13-16). Jesus only makes war to establish love, peace, and justice on earth.

v.20 the beast was captured: the Antichrist and False Prophet will be cast alive into the lake of fire at this time. The rest of the wicked will be cast in the lake of fire at the end of the Millennium (Rev. 20:11-15).

v.21 rest were killed: Jesus will kill the rest of the kings as prophesied by David in Psalm 110:5-6. After this battle, all Israel will receive Jesus as their Messiah and king (Mt. 23:39). The pinnacle of the second coming procession is Jesus' re-entry into the city of Jerusalem to be officially received by Israel.

13   He was clothed with a robe dipped in blood, and His name is called The Word of God.

14   And the armies in heaven, clothed in fine linen, white and clean, followed Him on white horses.

15   Now out of His mouth goes a sharp sword, that with it He should strike the nations. And He Himself will rule them with a rod of iron. He Himself treads the winepress of the fierceness and wrath of Almighty God.

16   And He has on His robe and on His thigh a name written:

KING OF KINGS AND LORD OF LORDS.

17   Then I saw an angel standing in the sun; and he cried with a loud voice, saying to all the birds that fly in the midst of heaven, "Come and gather together for the supper of the great God,

18   that you may eat the flesh of kings, the flesh of captains, the flesh of mighty men, the flesh of horses and of those who sit on them, and the flesh of all people, free and slave, both small and great."

19   And I saw the beast, the kings of the earth, and their armies, gathered together to make war against Him who sat on the horse and against His army.

20   Then the beast was captured, and with him the false prophet who worked signs in his presence, by which he deceived those who received the mark of the beast and those who worshiped his image. These two were cast alive into the lake of fire burning with brimstone.

21   And the rest were killed with the sword which proceeded from the mouth of Him who sat on the horse. And all the birds were filled with their flesh.

CHRONOLOGICAL SECTION #5

JUDGMENT   PROMISE   PERSECUTION   PRAYER/WORSHIP

REV. 20 The Millennium is a literal 1,000-year period in which Jesus will rule the earth.
v.2 there are four names of Satan: each name depicts different crimes and reveals ways in which Satan attacks us. *Dragon* denotes his cruelty. The *serpent* of old refers to the liar in the garden of Eden (Gen. 3). *Devil* means the accuser. *Satan* means the adversary who attacks us.

v.3 cast in the bottomless pit: Satan will be imprisoned for 1,000 years.

v.4 they sat on thrones: the saints of Revelation 19:14, 19 are the subject of the phrase "*they sat.*" Jesus will govern the earth in partnership with resurrected saints (Dan. 7:27; Mt. 19:28; 25:23; Lk. 19:17-19; 22:29-30; 1 Cor. 6:2-3; 2 Tim. 2:12; Rev. 2:26-27; 3:21; 5:10; 20:4-6; 22:5). At this time the kingdom of God will be openly manifest worldwide, affecting every sphere of life. The result will be a 1,000-year period of unprecedented blessing for the earth as Jesus establishes righteousness and prosperity, and restores the agriculture, atmosphere, and animal life to some of the conditions that were seen in the garden of Eden (Isa. 2:1-4; 9:6-7; 11:1-16; 51:1-8; 60-62; 65:17-25; Mt. 5:5; 6:10; 17:11; 19:28; Acts 3:21). *See page 126 for more on the Millennium*.

v.7 Satan released from prison: at the end of the Millennium, Satan will deceive the nations one last time. After 1,000 years in prison, Satan will be totally unchanged. Prison will not rehabilitate him because of the nature of pride and its refusal to repent. The rebellion at the end of the Millennium will show that people love sin more than God, regardless of their life circumstances. The Millennium was a perfect environment and yet after Satan's release, some in the nations will choose to rebel against Jesus with great hostility. One reason Jesus will allow Satan, "the snake," back into the garden as he was in Genesis 3 is because He wants the truth about the depravity of sin and pride and its incurable nature to be seen by all. At that time, no one will be able to blame their sin on their difficult circumstances because they will all have been living in the ideal environment of the Millennium. They will rebel because they love to sin. The necessity of eternal judgment will be understood at this time.

v.8 Gog and Magog: are prophetic titles of the demonically empowered world leader (Gog) and the nation (Magog) that he leads. Gog speaks of God's primary human adversary on the earth. The Antichrist is clearly the "Gog figure" in the Great Tribulation (Ezek. 38:2, 3, 14, 16, 18, 21; 39:1, 11, 15). However, at the end of the Millennium there will be a new "Gog figure" since the Antichrist will be in the lake of fire (Rev. 19:20); thus, they cannot be the same person.

CHRONOLOGICAL SECTION #5

20 Then I saw an angel coming down from heaven, having the key to the bottomless pit and a great chain in his hand.

2   He laid hold of the dragon, that serpent of old, who is the Devil and Satan, and bound him for a thousand years;

3   and he cast him into the bottomless pit, and shut him up, and set a seal on him, so that he should deceive the nations no more till the thousand years were finished. But after these things he must be released for a little while.

4   And I saw thrones, and they sat on them, and judgment was committed to them. Then I saw the souls of those who had been beheaded for their witness to Jesus and for the word of God, who had not worshiped the beast or his image, and had not received his mark on their foreheads or on their hands. And they lived and reigned with Christ for a thousand years.

5   But the rest of the dead did not live again until the thousand years were finished. This is the first resurrection.

6   Blessed and holy is he who has part in the first resurrection. Over such the second death has no power, but they shall be priests of God and of Christ, and shall reign with Him a thousand years.

7   Now when the thousand years have expired, Satan will be released from his prison

8   and will go out to deceive the nations which are in the four corners of the earth, Gog and Magog, to gather them together to battle, whose number is as the sand of the sea.

9   They went up on the breadth of the earth and surrounded the camp of the saints and the beloved city. And fire came down from God out of heaven and devoured them.

10   The devil, who deceived them, was cast into the lake of fire and brimstone where the beast and the false prophet are. And they will be tormented day and night forever and ever.

JUDGMENT   PROMISE   PERSECUTION   PRAYER/WORSHIP

v.11 great white throne: all *unbelievers* will be judged at the great white throne at the end of the 1,000 years. All *believers* are judged and rewarded at the judgment seat of Christ at the time of the seventh trumpet, immediately before the Millennium begins (1 Cor. 3:11-15; 2 Cor. 5:10).

v.11 white: speaks of God's purity and holiness (Ps. 97:2; Dan. 7:9).

v.12 books opened: all the deeds of the wicked are recorded in God's books.

v.14 Hades: all those in Hades will be cast into the lake of fire. The unrighteous dead in this age all go to Hades (hell), which functions as a temporary prison.

v.14 second death: the second death is to be permanently cast into the lake of fire, where all enjoyment of the positive qualities of *life* is forever absent.

REV. 21 **v.1 passed away:** theologians debate whether the *passing away* of this present earth means that it will be *annihilated* or *renovated* (renewed) after the Millennium. The Greek word for "pass away" is the same word that Paul used when he wrote: "If anyone is in Christ, he is a new creation; old things have passed away" (2 Cor. 5:17). On the day we were born again, old things in our life passed away. This does not mean that our humanity was *annihilated* but that it was *renewed* with salvation. I believe, in a similar way, that this earth will be *renovated*, not *annihilated.* The renewed earth will continue forever (1 Chr. 23:25, 28:8; Ps. 37:29; 78:69; 104:5; 105:10-11; 125:1-2; Isa. 60:21; Ezek. 37:25; Joel 3:20). The New Jerusalem will rest on the new earth forever.

v.2 coming down: the New Jerusalem will descend to the earth in two stages. Firstly, at the time of Jesus' return at the beginning of the Millennium (Rev. 21:10). Secondly, as a city on the new earth after the Millennium (Rev. 21:2). *The descent of the New Jerusalem in this verse is the last chronological event in Revelation.*

v.2 prepared and adorned: the New Jerusalem has been prepared as a place where all the saints will live forever in God's immediate presence. The Father adorns the city with great beauty; it can be compared to both the Holy of Holies and the garden of Eden.

v.3 tabernacle of God: the Father will dwell in face-to-face communion with human beings on the new earth forever. This is the high point of our salvation. God's purpose has always been to live together with His people on this earth.

v.5 write these words: the Father gives us a seven-fold message revealing His commitments to us (v. 5-8). This is only the second time in which the Father speaks in a direct way in Revelation (Rev. 1:8).

CHRONOLOGICAL SECTION #5

11   Then I saw a great white throne and Him who sat on it, from whose face the earth and the heaven fled away. And there was found no place for them.

12   And I saw the dead, small and great, standing before God, and books were opened. And another book was opened, which is the Book of Life. And the dead were judged according to their works, by the things which were written in the books.

13   The sea gave up the dead who were in it, and Death and Hades delivered up the dead who were in them. And they were judged, each one according to his works.

14   Then Death and Hades were cast into the lake of fire. This is the second death.

15   And anyone not found written in the Book of Life was cast into the lake of fire.

21 Now I saw a new heaven and a new earth, for the first heaven and the first earth had passed away. Also there was no more sea.

2   Then I, John, saw the holy city, New Jerusalem, coming down out of heaven from God, prepared as a bride adorned for her husband.

3   And I heard a loud voice from heaven saying, "Behold, the tabernacle of God is with men, and He will dwell with them, and they shall be His people. God Himself will be with them and be their God.

4   And God will wipe away every tear from their eyes; there shall be no more death, nor sorrow, nor crying. There shall be no more pain, for the former things have passed away."

5   Then He who sat on the throne said, "Behold, I make all things new." And He said to me, "Write, for these words are true and faithful."

JUDGMENT   PROMISE   PERSECUTION   PRAYER/WORSHIP

Angelic Explanation #5 gives us insight into the Bride's victory and the full restoration of God's purposes by describing the New Jerusalem in relationship to the millennial earth (Rev. 21:9-22:5). Jesus will restore to us all that He originally intended when He created the garden of Eden (Acts 3:19-21).

The angel who showed John the harlot Babylon (Rev. 17:1) also showed him the Bride (Rev. 21:9). They are parallel visions; both are clearly parenthetical sections in which the angel explains events that do not occur in chronological order. Revelation 21:9-22:5 is a parenthetical section, but its events do not occur until after the chronological events of Revelation 21:1-8. Revelation 21:9-22:5 describes the eternal and temporal realms together. We see the eternal state of the resurrected saints dwelling face to face with God, and the natural conditions of kings from the millennial earth who bring their glory into the city that has healing leaves for nations that still need healing (Rev. 21:22-27; 22:2).

Scripture shows that the New Jerusalem is close to millennial Jerusalem and accessible to people on earth, and yet not actually on earth. The dimensions of the New Jerusalem prohibit it from being physically on earth: millennial Jerusalem is about 10 square miles (Ezek. 48:30-35), whereas the New Jerusalem is 1,380 square miles (Rev. 21:16, *see page 90*). However, Scripture shows that people on earth are able to access the New Jerusalem. **Firstly**, the kings of the earth come into the New Jerusalem during the Millennium (Rev. 21:24-26). **Secondly**, the healing leaves in the New Jerusalem are for the millennial nations that need healing (Rev. 22:2). Thus, people on the millennial earth must have access to the healing leaves in the New Jerusalem (Rev. 22:2). **Thirdly**, angels guard the entry to the New Jerusalem to keep sinners out, as in Genesis 3:22-24 (Rev. 21:12).

v.9-21 John saw the New Jerusalem from two views: an **external view**, paralleling the Holy of Holies (Rev. 21:9-21), and an **internal view**, paralleling the garden of Eden (Rev. 21:22-22:5)

v. 9 Lamb's wife: His wife includes both the city and the saints who live in it.

v.10 New Jerusalem: will descend to the earth in two stages. It will first descend when Jesus returns to begin the Millennium (Rev. 21:10). When this happens, then *heaven is literally on earth*. It further descends after the Millennium when the earth is cleansed with fire to become the new earth (Rev. 21:2). The resurrected saints live here while they reign on the millennial earth.

6   And He said to me, "It is done! I am the Alpha and the Omega, the Beginning and the End. I will give of the fountain of the water of life freely to him who thirsts.

7   He who overcomes shall inherit all things, and I will be his God and he shall be My son.

8   But the cowardly, unbelieving, abominable, murderers, sexually immoral, sorcerers, idolaters, and all liars shall have their part in the lake which burns with fire and brimstone, which is the second death."

Angelic Explanation #5: The **RESTORATION** of All Things (Acts 3:21)

9   Then one of the seven angels who had the seven bowls filled with the seven last plagues came to me and talked with me, saying, "Come, I will show you the bride, the Lamb's wife."

10   And he carried me away in the Spirit to a great and high mountain, and showed me the great city, the holy Jerusalem, descending out of heaven from God,

11   having the glory of God. Her light was like a most precious stone, like a jasper stone, clear as crystal.

12   Also she had a great and high wall with twelve gates, and twelve angels at the gates, and names written on them, which are the names of the twelve tribes of the children of Israel:

13   three gates on the east, three gates on the north, three gates on the south, and three gates on the west.

14   Now the wall of the city had twelve foundations, and on them were the names of the twelve apostles of the Lamb.

15   And he who talked with me had a gold reed to measure the city, its gates, and its wall.

ANGELIC EXPLANATION #5

JUDGMENT   PROMISE   PERSECUTION   PRAYER/WORSHIP

v.16 laid out as a square: the city's design is described as a cube (21:16), like the Holy of Holies in Solomon's temple (1 Kgs. 6:20).

v.16 twelve thousand furlongs: approximately 1,380 miles in length, height, and width. A furlong is a Greek measurement that was approximately 600 feet or about one-eighth of a mile. Outer space is 800 miles from earth.

v.17 walls: are 144 cubits or 216 feet or 72 yards thick. A cubit was about 18 inches. The walls are made with precious stones like those on the breastplate of the high priest (Ex. 28:17-20; 39:10; Rev. 21:18-20).

v.18 construction of jasper: ancient jasper had diamond-like transparency.

v.19 foundations: eight of the precious stones (21:19-20) were also found on the high priest's breastplate signifying nearness to God (Ex. 28:17-20; 39:10).

v.21 gates: if each side of the city is 1,380 miles long, then there are almost 500 miles between each of the twelve gates.

In Revelation 21:22-22:5, John gives an **internal view** of the city as the garden of Eden. He describes the city's beauty (21:22-27) and its life with face-to-face communion with God (22:1-5). It is a worshiping city with no temple (21:22; 22:4a); an illuminated city with no sun (21:23; 22:5); a governmental city with God's throne (21:24, 26; 22:3-5d); a servant city that works (21:25b; 22:3c, 5a); and a holy city without any sin (21:27, 8; 22:14-15).

We know Revelation 21:22-27 refers to the Millennium because John describes people on millennial earth interacting with the New Jerusalem. He mentioned things in the natural and temporal realm that normally do not interact with the eternal state. For example, we see the eternal state of the resurrected saints in the New Jerusalem and the natural conditions of kings on the millennial earth, who bring their glory into the city and receive the leaves that heal the nations on the millennial earth. The occupants of this city are described in their eternal state, possessing their eternal inheritance.

v.24 kings of the earth: the millennial kings will come into the New Jerusalem to offer the glory and honor of their nation to Jesus.

v.27 nothing that defiles can enter: angels guard the entry to the city to keep sinners out (Rev. 21:12, 27; 22:14-15). Angels guarded the entrance to the garden of Eden after Adam sinned (Gen. 3:22-24).

ANGELIC EXPLANATION #5

16   The city is laid out as a square; its length is as great as its breadth. And he measured the city with the reed: twelve thousand furlongs. Its length, breadth, and height are equal.

17   Then he measured its wall: one hundred and forty-four cubits, according to the measure of a man, that is, of an angel.

18   The construction of its wall was of jasper; and the city was pure gold, like clear glass.

19   The foundations of the wall of the city were adorned with all kinds of precious stones: the first foundation was jasper, the second sapphire, the third chalcedony, the fourth emerald,

20   the fifth sardonyx, the sixth sardius, the seventh chrysolite, the eighth beryl, the ninth topaz, the tenth chrysoprase, the eleventh jacinth, and the twelfth amethyst.

21   The twelve gates were twelve pearls: each individual gate was of one pearl. And the street of the city was pure gold, like transparent glass.

22   But I saw no temple in it, for the Lord God Almighty and the Lamb are its temple.

23   The city had no need of the sun or of the moon to shine in it, for the glory of God illuminated it. The Lamb is its light.

24   And the nations of those who are saved shall walk in its light, and the kings of the earth bring their glory and honor into it.

25   Its gates shall not be shut at all by day (there shall be no night there).

26   And they shall bring the glory and the honor of the nations into it.

27   But there shall by no means enter it anything that defiles, or causes an abomination or a lie, but only those who are written in the Lamb's Book of Life.

JUDGMENT   PROMISE   PERSECUTION   PRAYER/WORSHIP

REV. 22 Revelation 22:1-5 describes life in the holy city in a way that is parallel to the garden of Eden with the *river of life* (v. 1) and the *tree of life* (v. 2), *without a curse* (v. 3), as the saints serve *God in a face-to-face relationship* (v. 4). Adam and Eve experienced these blessings in Eden before they sinned (Gen. 3).

v.1 river of life: pure water that imparts life to those who drink it.

v.2 healing of the nations: the leaves will be used in the process of healing the millennial nations. Therefore these nations must have access to them.

v.3 no curse: on the cross, Jesus became a curse for us, thereby removing the curse of our sin from us (Gal. 3:13). The fullness of life without the curse will be enjoyed forever in the city.

v.3 the throne of the Lamb: Jesus' throne is in the New Jerusalem. It is also in Jerusalem on the millennial earth (Jer. 3:17). This does not imply that Jesus has two thrones, but that there are two expressions of His one throne, referred to as His throne of glory (Mt. 25:31), which connects the heavenly and earthly realms.

v.4 see His face: the saints shall serve God in a face-to-face relationship filled with holiness. The saints will not be idle but will be administrating His government with authority over all God's creation.

v.4 His name: to have the name of God written on one's forehead is to receive greater revelation of His heart and beauty. To receive a new name from God means to receive new aspects of our identity, with new abilities and a new ministry assignment in the age to come.

v.7 keeps the prophecy: blessing is promised to any who will keep the prophecy, which includes fully agreeing with the book of Revelation. *See the article "Keeping the Words of the Prophecy" on page 9*. To keep it includes engaging in the actual battle plan in prayer and proclamation even unto death. There is only one generation who will keep (walk out) the battle plan on a global level and thus hasten the day of the Lord (2 Pet. 3:12).

v.10 do not seal the words: God did not seal the book of Revelation because He wants us to understand its meaning in this age.

v.11 let him be unjust still: the fundamental nature of a person will not change in the age to come. The wicked will become more wicked and the righteous will continue in righteousness forever. There will be no rehabilitation from sin in the lake of fire.

ANGELIC EXPLANATION #5

22 And he showed me a pure river of water of life, clear as crystal, proceeding from the throne of God and of the Lamb.

2   In the middle of its street, and on either side of the river, was the tree of life, which bore twelve fruits, each tree yielding its fruit every month. The leaves of the tree were for the healing of the nations.

3   And there shall be no more curse, but the throne of God and of the Lamb shall be in it, and His servants shall serve Him.

4   They shall see His face, and His name shall be on their foreheads.

5   There shall be no night there: They need no lamp nor light of the sun, for the Lord God gives them light. And they shall reign forever and ever.

6   Then he said to me, "These words are faithful and true." And the Lord God of the holy prophets sent His angel to show His servants the things which must shortly take place.

7   "Behold, I am coming quickly! Blessed is he who keeps the words of the prophecy of this book."

8   Now I, John, saw and heard these things. And when I heard and saw, I fell down to worship before the feet of the angel who showed me these things.

9   Then he said to me, "See that you do not do that. For I am your fellow servant, and of your brethren the prophets, and of those who keep the words of this book. Worship God."

10   And he said to me, "Do not seal the words of the prophecy of this book, for the time is at hand.

11   He who is unjust, let him be unjust still; he who is filthy, let him be filthy still; he who is righteous, let him be righteous still; he who is holy, let him be holy still."

JUDGMENT   PROMISE   PERSECUTION   PRAYER/WORSHIP

v.12 My reward: the saints are rewarded at the seventh trumpet (Rev. 11:18).

v.14 enter through the gates into the city: the godly on the millennial earth can enter the New Jerusalem; unbelievers are on the outside (v. 15).

v.16 Root and Offspring: Jesus is the **Root** that supports and brings life to all that God promised to Israel in relation to the throne of David. Jesus is the **Root** that existed long before David; thus He is *fully God*. Jesus is the **Offspring** of David because He was born into David's family line; thus He is *fully man*.

v.16 Bright Star: Jesus will guide His people in the deep darkness of the Tribulation (Isa. 60:1). The beauty of His brightness fascinates His people.

v.16 Morning Star: Jesus will give assurance of victory to His people in the darkest time of human history. The morning star is the brightest star in the sky that is seen just before the dawning of a new day. Jesus will come as the sure sign that the *dawning of the "millennial day" is at hand* (2 Pet. 3:8). Jesus was prophesied to be the star or king from Jacob's family line who would be given dominion over the nations (Num. 24:17-19).

v.17 Spirit and the Bride: this is one of the most significant prophecies in the Bible, which describes the end-time Church in the generation the Lord returns. This is the only time in history that the Church worldwide will be doing and saying the same thing as the Holy Spirit. We will be in unity with the Spirit in four ways:
- Anointed with the Spirit
- Engaged in intercession
- Established in our bridal identity
- Effective in the harvest

v.17 Come: we will cry "**come**" in two different directions.

Firstly, we cry out vertically to Jesus in *intercession* to **come to us** in three ways:
- Come *near us* in intimacy: grant a breakthrough for my heart
- Come *to us* in revival: grant a breakthrough for my city or nation
- Come *for us* in the sky: grant a breakthrough in history

Secondly, we cry out horizontally in *proclamation* to people to **come to Jesus**:
- That *unbelievers* would come to Jesus: evangelism
- That *believers* would come to Jesus: renewal
- That *governments* would come to Jesus: transformation

v.18 adds to these things: God promises to judge any who add or subtract anything from this prophecy.

ANGELIC EXPLANATION #5

12   "And behold, I am coming quickly, and My reward is with Me, to give to every one according to his work.

13   I am the Alpha and the Omega, the Beginning and the End, the First and the Last."

14   Blessed are those who do His commandments, that they may have the right to the tree of life, and may enter through the gates into the city.

15   But outside are dogs and sorcerers and sexually immoral and murderers and idolaters, and whoever loves and practices a lie.

16   "I, Jesus, have sent My angel to testify to you these things in the churches. I am the Root and the Offspring of David, the Bright and Morning Star."

17   And the Spirit and the bride say, "Come!" And let him who hears say, "Come!" And let him who thirsts come. Whoever desires, let him take the water of life freely.

18   For I testify to everyone who hears the words of the prophecy of this book: If anyone adds to these things, God will add to him the plagues that are written in this book;

19   and if anyone takes away from the words of the book of this prophecy, God shall take away his part from the Book of Life, from the holy city, and from the things which are written in this book.

20   He who testifies to these things says, "Surely I am coming quickly."

Amen. Even so, come, Lord Jesus!

21   The grace of our Lord Jesus Christ be with you all. Amen.

JUDGMENT   PROMISE   PERSECUTION   PRAYER/WORSHIP

WHY STUDY THE END TIMES?

Jesus said that no one knows the day or the hour of His return. However, I believe that the Church in the generation of His return will know that they are in the final generation of natural history. It is my personal belief that we are currently in the beginning stages of that generation. I do not have a personal revelation from God about this. Rather, I conclude this by observation of the prophetic signs of the times that are mentioned in the Scriptures. I do not know if the final events will begin in five years or fifty years. My guess is that it will be closer to fifty years than five years.

Firstly, the generation in which the Lord returns will be announced with prophetic signs. These signs are meant to be understood and paid attention to. They will increase in intensity as we get closer to Jesus' return. The scriptural prophetic signs include signs in the heavens, in nature (earthquakes, etc.), and in social, political, military, religious, scientific, technological, and economic developments. Jesus and Paul exhorted those in the generation that Jesus returns to know the prophetic signs (Mt. 24:32-34; Lk. 21:25-29; 1 Thes. 5:1-6; 2 Thes. 2:1-11).

> *Now learn this parable from the fig tree: When its branch has already become tender and puts forth leaves, you know that summer is near. So you also, when you see all these things, know that it is near—at the doors! (Mt. 24:32-33)*

The prophetic signs that are outlined in Scripture will serve God's people like a weather station that signals trouble ahead of time so that people can prepare. The example of the Southeast Asia tsunami on December 26, 2004, illustrates this. Several hundred thousand people died. Many lives could have been saved simply by knowing an hour earlier that the tsunami was coming.

Jesus rebuked Israel for being unable to read the prophetic signs at His first coming. He told Israel that they would experience God's judgment for being unresponsive to Him. This was partially due to Israel not knowing the time of their visitation from God.

Hypocrites! You know how to discern the face of the sky, but you cannot discern the signs of the times. (Mt. 16:3)

For days will come . . . when your enemies will . . . level you, and your children to the ground . . . because you did not know the time of your visitation. (Lk. 19:43-44)

Secondly, the generation the Lord returns will be the most dramatic and important time in history. There will be two great extremes that unfold in one generation: the greatest revival and the most severe pressures in society (the Great Tribulation). We must be informed about what the Scripture says about the generation that will witness such dramatic and important events.

Thirdly, Jesus spoke more about the last generation of natural history than any other generation. Thus, we should pay close attention to what the Scripture says it. There are over 150 chapters in the Bible that focus on the end times. Compare this to the four gospels, which total 89 chapters. The gospels give us a record of Jesus' ministry related to His first coming when He redeemed us from our sins. The 150 chapters on the end times reveal His ministry related to His second coming when He will rule all the nations. Many of God's people neglect these 150 chapters without considering that they come from the same Bible, reveal the same Jesus, and manifest the same power of the Spirit as the four gospels.

FOUR COMMON MISCONCEPTIONS RELATED TO END-TIME PROPHECY
Firstly, it is a misconception to believe that the majority in the Church in **every generation believed that they were the final generation**. It is true that in many generations less than 1% of the Church thought they were in the end times. However, 99% did not believe it. Only in the generation of the early apostles was there a sustained conviction among the majority of God's people that they would see the return of Jesus. Today, this same universal conviction is beginning to happen again in the Body of Christ. If it continues, it will be only the second time in church history that this has occurred in a universal and sustained way.

Secondly, it is a misconception to believe that end-time prophecy *is not relevant* to our lives. Gaining understanding about the end times is practical in being prepared to be victorious in the most dramatic hour of human history.

Thirdly, it is a misconception to believe that the events and numbers in the book of Revelation are to be ***interpreted symbolically*** instead of taken in their plain, literal meaning, unless the passages itself indicates that it is to be interpreted symbolically, as is the case in Revelation 1:20; 5:6; 11:8; 12:1, 3, 9; and 17:7, 9.

Fourthly, it is a misconception to believe that end-time prophecies ***are impossible to understand*** except by scholars. God gave the Bible to be understood by all.

THE BENEFITS OF UNDERSTANDING THE END TIMES

Certainty of victory: The Church will be victorious in love during the most dramatic hour of history. God is fully in control of the end-time crisis. He is never surprised. The result of knowing His plans for end times is to grow in peace instead of being overcome with fear about it. When God's people see the scriptural signs of the times fulfilled before their eyes, it will give them confidence that God is in control and that victory is certain. This will help them to persevere instead of drawing back in compromise, and it will give them courage to proclaim the message to others.

Direction: Having a compass in a storm at sea is an issue of life and death. Similarly, by understanding the end-time Scriptures, we can have right expectations for what is coming, and be emotionally prepared with right expectations. We will need understanding to avoid the seductions and temptations of the enemy. For example, by understanding the end-time Scriptures, we are alerted to the evil economic and religious enterprises of the harlot Babylon that will seem good to those who lack discernment.

Urgency: With understanding of the end-time scriptures, we grow in faith that our intercession will minimize evil and increase victory (Joel 2:12-18). Moses' prayers both released as well as stopped God's judgments (Ex. 7-12). Our prayers can release God's protection. Understanding the end-time scriptures gives us urgency to live a life of prayer and to go deep in the things of God.

HOW TO INTERPRET THE BOOK OF REVELATION

The book of Revelation is titled the Revelation of Jesus because it reveals His heart, power, and leadership (Rev. 1:1). If we read it with a devotional spirit, it will cause us to trust and adore Jesus.

Some wrongly conclude that no one can understand the book of Revelation. The truth is that it was written to be understood by all of God's people. The Father gave it as a gift to His Church. It was written in a straightforward way. It says what it means and means what it says. It was written for the majority of people throughout history. Most of them have been uneducated, yet God gave it specifically to them.

The book of Revelation says what it means
and means what it says

The events and numbers in Revelation are to be understood in their plain or literal meaning. For instance, when Revelation states that one-fourth of the earth will be killed, it means that literally 25 percent of the earth will die (Rev. 6:8). When it states that hail and fire mingled with blood will fall from heaven, we are meant to understand this in its plain sense (Rev. 8:7). When John wrote about Jesus' 1,000-year reign on earth, he referred to a literal 1,000-year period (Rev. 20:4-6).

Whenever something is meant to be interpreted symbolically, John clearly indicates it as in Revelation 1:20; 5:6; 11:8; 12:1, 3, 9; 17:7, 9. Most of the symbols found in Revelation are interpreted in the context of the book itself, or else they are clearly interpreted in other parts of Scripture. For example, Daniel used some of the same symbols as John (Dan. 7-12). There are seven main symbols in the book of Revelation. Each one is clearly interpreted by the Scripture itself. When we understand that many of the symbols are explained in Scripture and that this book is to be understood plainly and in a straightforward way, then we find motivation to study this book with diligence.

In this study guide, we approach the book of Revelation through a perspective that will be new to some of our readers. Revelation is first and foremost about the unveiling of Jesus as prophet, priest, and king at the beginning of the book, and then as bridegroom, king, and judge at the end. As we see more of the majesty and beauty of Jesus through reading this book, our hearts will be energized as we walk in a deeper intimacy with God.

The book of Revelation serves as:

- Jesus' strategic battle plan to confront the Antichrist and drive evil off the planet
- The Church's canonized prayer manual to release judgment on the Antichrist in the way that Moses released judgments on Pharaoh
- The Father's blueprint of love that He will use to prepare the Bride in the end times

For some, the book of Revelation is perceived as a book that primarily describes God's wrath on the Church. Therefore, they hope to leave the earth in the rapture to escape the trouble. However, the book of Revelation describes the praying Church partnering with Jesus to release God's judgment on the Antichrist's evil empire. Just as Moses released the ten plagues on Pharaoh, so the book of Revelation depicts the praying Church releasing God's judgments on the Antichrist, a type of end-time Pharaoh.

The book of Revelation is about Jesus returning to take leadership of the earth in deep partnership with the end-time praying Church. The book is Jesus' battle plan to confront the Antichrist and to destroy all the evil governments on earth by His judgments, as seen in the Great Tribulation (Rev. 6-19). The book of Revelation helps to prepare the Church to offer global *unified prayers of faith* that will bind evil and loose Jesus' power (Mt. 16:18-19).

> *I will build My church, and the gates of Hades shall not prevail against it. I will give you the keys of the kingdom . . . and whatever you bind on earth will be bound in heaven, and whatever you loose on earth will be loosed in heaven. (Mt. 16:18-19)*

We must not think of ourselves as *victims* who are seeking to *escape* the Great Tribulation; rather, we must see ourselves as *participants*, under Jesus' leadership, who seek to *release* the Great Tribulation on the Antichrist's empire.

I refer to Revelation as the *end-time book of Acts*. Whereas the book of Acts describes the activity of the Holy Spirit that was released through the early church, the book of Revelation describes the power of the Holy Spirit that will be released through the end-time Church. This end-time book of Acts is Jesus' action plan to take over the earth; it is His blueprint, or His story line, of love. His judgments will be released to remove everything that hinders love. One key to understanding Revelation is to understand its structure, which consists of main four parts (Rev. 1; Rev. 2-3; Rev. 4-5; and Rev. 6-22). The fourth part (Rev. 6-22) has five **chronological sections** (Rev. 6:1-17; 8:1-9:21; 11:15-18; 15:1-16:21; 19:11-21:8), and five **angelic explanations** (Rev. 7:1-17; 10:1-11:14; 12:1-14:20; 17:1-19:10; 21:9-22:5). As we understand the relationship between the **chronological sections** and the **angelic explanations**, the book of Revelation becomes easier to understand.

The chronological sections focus on the judgments that God will release during the Great Tribulation. They tell the main story line as it unfolds on the earth in a sequential way. In other words, the judgment events are described as they occur, one after the other, in chronological order. For example, after the first seal comes the second seal, which in turn is followed by the third seal, and so on.

The angelic explanations describe **what Satan will do** in his attacks against the Church and what **God will do to** help the saints (with power, protection, direction, or reward).

In these explanations, the angel puts the story line "on pause" to answer the questions that emerge as a result of the severity of God's judgments. The two main questions that are answered are "Why are God's judgments in the chronological sections so severe?" and "What will happen to God's people?" In these angelic explanations, the angel gives John insight in order to strengthen and comfort the end-time Church by answering these questions.

PRAYING THE THIRTY DESCRIPTIONS OF JESUS IN REVELATION 1-3

In Revelation 1-3, Jesus highlights thirty specific descriptions of His majesty, ministry, and personality. We can identify them from Jesus' names, appearance, actions, and clothing. Each description is intentional and communicates a clear message about Jesus. For example, the garments that He wears speak of Him as a high priest; His eyes of fire reveal that He is a prophet. Revelation 1-3 is the most complete picture of Jesus in the Bible. These thirty descriptions give us insight into *who He is* (how He thinks and feels) and *what He will do* in His plan to cleanse the earth from evil. If we read it with the right perspective, it inspires us to adore Jesus and trust His leadership.

There are twenty-four descriptions in Revelation 1 and eighteen in Revelation 2-3, totaling forty-two. Since twelve are used in both Revelation 1 and Revelation 2-3, there are thirty distinct descriptions.

> *From Jesus Christ, the faithful witness, the firstborn from the dead, and the ruler over the kings of the earth. To Him who loved us and washed us from our sins in His own blood, and has made us kings and priests to His God and Father . . . Behold, He is coming with clouds . . . I heard behind me a loud voice, as of a trumpet, saying, "I am the Alpha and the Omega, the First and the Last," and, "What you see, write in a book and send it to the seven churches" . . . Having turned I saw seven golden lampstands, and in the midst of the seven lampstands One like the Son of Man, clothed with a garment down to the feet and girded about the chest with a golden band. His head and hair were white like wool, as white as snow, and His eyes like a flame of fire; His feet were like fine brass, as if refined in a furnace, and His voice as the sound of many waters; He had in His right hand seven stars, out of His mouth went a sharp two-edged sword, and His countenance was like the sun shining in its strength. When I saw Him, I fell at His feet as dead. But He laid His right hand on me, saying to me, "Do not be afraid; I am the First and the Last. I am He who lives, and was dead, and behold, I am alive forevermore. Amen. I have the keys of Hades and of Death." (Rev. 1:5-18)*

He who holds the seven stars . . . walks in the midst of the seven lampstands . . . The First and the Last, who was dead, and came to life . . . He who has the sharp two-edged sword . . . The Son of God, who has eyes like a flame of fire, and His feet like fine brass . . . He who has the seven Spirits of God and the seven stars . . . I will come upon you as a thief . . . He who is holy, He who is true, He who has the key of David . . . The Amen, the faithful and true witness, the beginning of the creation of God (Rev. 2:1-3:14)

We can apply these thirty truths about Jesus to our lives in three ways, according to the acronym **A-R-K**.

Agreement: Make declarations of *agreement* to Jesus about who He is and what He does. We declare each truth back to Jesus with affection and gratitude.

Revelation: Pray for increased *revelation* of each description (Eph. 1:17).

The Father of glory may give to you the spirit of wisdom and revelation in the knowledge of Him. (Eph. 1:17)

Keep the prophecy: Resolve to *keep* each of the thirty truths by responding in faith and obedience to each truth in our actions and attitudes, and by asking for the Spirit's help to be faithful.

Blessed is he who keeps the words of the prophecy of this book . . . I (angel) am your fellow servant, and . . . of those who keep the words of this book. (Rev. 22:7-9, comment added)

EXAMPLES OF PRAYING ACCORDING TO THE A-R-K PRINCIPLE

Jesus is the faithful witness: He spoke the truth regardless of what it cost.
Agreement: *"Jesus, You are the faithful witness to the truth. You are the truth. I thank You that You always tell the truth. I love this about You. I trust what You say. You are reliable. You took a stand that cost Your reputation and life."*
Revelation: *"Reveal Yourself to me as the faithful witness."*
Keep the prophecy: *"I commit to speak the truth regardless of what it costs, as the Spirit leads me. I trust what You say. Help me to walk this truth out."*

Jesus is the firstborn from the dead: He is preeminent over all.
Agreement: *"Your are the firstborn. I rejoice in Your preeminence over all."*
Revelation: *"Reveal Yourself to me as the firstborn. Teach me more about this."*
Keep the prophecy: *"I will serve You in a way that draws others to You, not me. Help me live in humility so that people are attracted to You, not me. I set my heart to live in the spirit of a friend of the Bridegroom (Jn. 3:29). Help me in this, Lord."*

We do not preach ourselves, but Christ Jesus the Lord... (2 Cor. 4:5)

Jesus is the ruler over the kings of the earth: All kings will submit to Him.
Agreement: *"Jesus, You are the ruler over all the kings on earth. All the kings on earth and through history will bow before You. I love Your greatness over all men."*
Revelation: *"Reveal Yourself to me as the ruler of all kings."*
Keep the prophecy: *"I will submit to Your great leadership. Empower me to obey You. Help me to walk this out. I will work to call kings and those in authority to obey You regardless of what it costs me."*

Jesus is the Son of Man: He is fully God and fully man.
Agreement: *"Jesus, You are the Son of Man. You are fully God and fully man. I love this about You. You became a man to win me. I trust Your leadership."*
Revelation: *"Reveal Yourself to me and show me Your glory as the Son of Man."*
Keep the prophecy: *"I commit to proclaim who You are as the One who rules the nations. I will obey You and submit to Your great leadership. Empower me to obey You. Help me to walk this out."*

FOUR DESIGNATIONS FOR THE LAST THREE AND A HALF YEARS

There are eight scriptures and four different phrases that describe the final three and a half years before Jesus' return. Different terminology is used so that the meaning is clear and that no one will be able to dismiss this prophetic time frame as symbolic.

This time period is referred to twice as *1,260 days* (Rev. 11:3; 12:6); twice as *42 months* (Rev. 11:2; 13:5); three times as *"time, times, and half a time"* (Rev. 12:14; Dan. 7:25; 12:7); and once as *"the middle of the week"* (Dan. 9:27—a Hebrew week was a seven-year period; thus, the middle of it speaks of three and a half years).

Compare the following passages to see the different terminology used to describe the Antichrist's oppression of the Church and Israel for three and a half years. For example, the Antichrist will be given authority to continue against Israel and the Church for 42 months. (Rev. 13:5). The Gentiles under the Antichrist's leadership will oppress Jerusalem for 42 months (Rev. 11:2).

- The two witnesses prophesy in Jerusalem for *1,260 days* (Rev. 11:3). The remnant of Israel will be hidden from the Antichrist in the wilderness for *1,260 days* (Rev. 12:6) which is also described as *time, times, and half a time* (Rev. 12:14).

- The Antichrist will be given authority to continue against the saints for *time, times, and half a time* or three and a half years (Dan. 7:25). Israel's strength will be completely shattered after three and half years or *time, times, and half a time* (Dan. 12:7). The term *time* refers to one year, *times* refers to two years, and *half a time* speaks of half a year.

After three and half years of "great trouble" the nations see the sign of the Son of Man in the sky (Mt. 24:29-31).

Immediately after this, the Antichrist's focus will change from persecuting Israel and the Church to rallying the nations to make war against Jesus (Rev. 17:14; 19:11, 19).

THE SIGNIFICANCE OF JESUS' SEVEN LETTERS TO THE SEVEN CHURCHES

In Revelation 2 and 3, Jesus gives John a message for seven churches in Asia Minor (Ephesus, Smyrna, Pergamos, Thyatira, Sardis, Philadelphia, and Laodicea). John was instructed to write out the messages and send them as a letter.

These seven letters were given to strengthen the churches in John's day and throughout church history. However, their most important application is yet future.

The issues that Jesus addresses in the churches of John's day were strategically selected to help them; additionally, they are to prepare the end-time Church to stand against sinful seductions and fierce persecutions that will have striking similarities to the time of the seven churches. Thus, the seven letters identify the most important issues that will challenge the faith and obedience of the end-time Church.

These seven letters give us a clear portrait of what Jesus requires of the Church, to whom He will entrust great power so we may partner with Him in His end-time battle plan (Rev. 6-22).

By overcoming in these specific areas, the Church will possess the maturity in love, purity, and wisdom that will be necessary to fully partner with Jesus in the great end-time revival. In these letters, Jesus defined spiritual maturity, or what it means to love God and people and to be prepared as His Bride (Rev. 19:8).

In Revelation 1-3, Jesus highlights thirty different aspects of His majesty and twenty-two specific rewards that overcomers will receive as a prize for their faithfulness. Each of the seven letters begins with Jesus emphasizing specific aspects of His majesty.

Jesus declared the truths in these letters to be of great importance by repeatedly saying: "He who has an ear, let him hear what the Spirit says to the churches."

This is the exhortation that Jesus repeated most in His earthly ministry. It is recorded sixteen times (eight times in the gospels and eight times in Revelation (Mt. 11:15; 13:9, 43; Mk. 4:9, 23; 7:16; Lk. 8:8; 14:35; Rev. 2:7, 11, 17, 29; 3:6, 13, 22; 13:9). **Firstly**, this saying signals that the truth being proclaimed is extremely important to Jesus. **Secondly**, it calls us to pay careful attention to what it says. Jesus is saying that there is more than what is immediately obvious and that it will require diligence to grasp its full implications. **Thirdly**, we will need the help of the Holy Spirit to grasp its truth. The unaided mind of one who reads it will not automatically comprehend the truth being set forth.

The "angel" of the church refers to the main apostolic leader over each church. The word *angel* is *angelos* in Greek. In the New Testament, this word means *messenger* and can refer to either an angelic or human messenger (Lk. 7:24, 27; 9:52). It was translated "messenger" when referring to John the Baptist (Mt. 11:10; Mk. 1:2). In Revelation 2-3, it refers to a human messenger or the apostolic leader of the church in that city. This "messenger" was responsible to guard the message and keep it from being distorted through compromise, fear, or neglect.

This passage gives us the most in-depth detail on eternal rewards in all of Scripture. Jesus promised twenty-two eternal rewards to motivate His people to persevere until the end. To overcome means to walk in spiritual maturity by consistently *seeking* to walk in obedience. Overcoming does not mean attaining perfection in our character but constantly *reaching* for wholehearted obedience.

The rewards in Revelation 2-3 are given in differing degrees according to the faithfulness of the overcomers in loving and obeying Jesus. Rewards are given in addition to the free gift of eternal life. Jesus is speaking to churches. The issue of salvation is settled; the issue in focus is the particular areas of unfaithfulness that Jesus emphasizes in their lives. There will be a vast difference in the measure of glory of each believer's reward.

See page 108 for more on rewards and being an overcomer.

OVERCOMERS WHO RECEIVE REWARDS IN REVELATION 2-3

In Revelation 2-3, Jesus speaks of twenty-two rewards that are given to motivate and stabilize His people during the end times.

THE TWENTY-TWO REWARDS

- To eat from the tree of life in the midst of Paradise (2:7)
- To receive the crown of life (2:10)
- To not be hurt by the second death (2:11)
- To eat hidden manna (2:17)
- To receive a white stone (2:17)
- To receive a new name written on the stone (2:17)
- To have power over the nations (2:26)
- To receive the morning star (2:28)
- To receive white garments (Rev 3:5)
- To receive a name that is not blotted from the Book of Life (3:5)
- For Jesus to confess their names before the Father and angels (3:5)
- For their persecutors to worship before their feet (3:9)
- For their persecutors to know that Jesus loves them (3:9)
- To be made a pillar in God's temple (3:12)
- To have the Father's name written on them (3:12)
- To have Jesus' new name written on them (3:12)
- To have the name of the New Jerusalem written on them (3:12)
- To receive gold to make them rich (3:18)
- To receive white garments, that their shame not be revealed (3:18)
- To have anointed eyes to see more (3:18)
- To eat with Jesus (3:20)
- To sit on His Throne (3:21)

In Revelation 2-3, Jesus is speaking to churches. He was not exhorting them to be born again. He was speaking to believers who had already received the free gift of salvation based on Jesus' work on the cross (Eph. 2:8-9). The issue of salvation was settled for these churches. Rewards are given based on our works. He was offering born-again believers rewards as incentives to greater diligence. There will be a difference in the measure of glory that each believer will be rewarded (1 Cor. 15:41-42). The rewards of chapters 2 and 3 are given in different degrees according to a believer's faithfulness in loving and obeying Jesus. Not all Christians overcome the specific unfaithfulness Jesus highlights in these chapters. Most of these twenty-two rewards will be received by all believers in at least an introductory way. The issue here pertains to what measure of the reward a believer receives. Only overcomers will receive the *fullest measure* of these rewards.

John spoke of overcomers in two different contexts (Rev. 2-3; 1 Jn. 4-5)

Context #1: Overcoming worldly unbelief: All believers overcome in this general way. John wrote of overcoming the world (1 Jn. 5:4-5). One overcomes in this context by believing in Jesus and refusing the heresies that John confronted in his epistle, namely, the Antichrist teachings that said Jesus was not God and did not come in the flesh. This was a call to overcome deception by believing in Jesus as fully God and fully man and refusing to believe lies about Him.

Context #2: Overcoming unfaithfulness: Not all believers overcome in this specific way. John wrote of overcoming areas of unfaithfulness in a believer's life as specifically defined in different ways in each of the seven letters to the churches in Revelation (Rev. 2-3). To overcome means to walk in spiritual maturity or to be consistent in obedience (2 Thes. 1:10-11).

As unbelievers, we *overcome unbelief* and the world on the day we become born-again Christians (1 Jn. 5:4-5). As believers, we *overcome unfaithfulness* in our lives only after we endure in obedience until the end of our life. An overcomer, in this context, is one who matures in the specific areas of faithfulness that Jesus emphasized in his life.

HOW TO INTERPRET THE SEALS, TRUMPETS, AND BOWLS

The book of Revelation describes three sets of divine judgments, i.e., seven seals (Rev. 6), seven trumpets (Rev. 8-9), and seven bowls of wrath (Rev. 15-16). These twenty-one judgment events will be released against the harlot Babylon religion and/or the Antichrist's empire during the Great Tribulation. They will occur at the same time in which the Church experiences the greatest revival in history. God's judgments in the Great Tribulation will not be poured out on the saints. God did not appoint the saints to wrath, but to obtain salvation through Jesus (1 Thes. 5:9).

These judgments will be literal events that must not be explained away symbolically. Our method of interpretation is the plain, literal, commonsense approach. Each of these judgments are future events; they have not yet occurred in history. This is known as the futurist view. There are three other views of these judgments that are promoted today. They are the preterist view, the historicist view, and the idealist view. Though I honor the godly people who teach these views, I reject each of these three views. The preterist view sees most of Revelation as having been fulfilled in the events related to the destruction of Jerusalem in 70 AD and the fall of Rome (in the first three centuries after Jesus' death). The historicist view interprets Revelation as a progressive unfolding of events throughout church history. Thus, they see many of these prophecies as being partially fulfilled in history yet with a greater fulfillment in the end times. The idealist view interprets Revelation as a symbolic picture of the spiritual conflict between good and evil that has been occurring all throughout history. This view does not see a special end-time application of the book of Revelation.

The twenty-one judgment events are redemptive. We can see this in two ways. Firstly, they will result in unbelievers crying out to Jesus for mercy and salvation. The purpose of His judgments is to remove all that hinders love in the nations, and to bring people to Jesus. God will use the least severe judgments to reach the greatest number of people at the deepest level of love. Secondly, they will hinder the people in the Antichrist's empire in their zeal to persecute the saints and to promote their sinful lifestyles.

The judgments are numbered, giving the saints the knowledge of the chronological order in which they will unfold on the earth. For example, the first seal will be followed by the second seal which in turn will be followed by the third one, and so on. This will have a practical application in allowing the Church to prophesy and pray for the release of these judgment events in the order that God has ordained.

The three series of judgments (seals, trumpets, and bowls) are progressive in that they will increase in intensity as each series is released. The seal judgment events will be surpassed in severity by the trumpet judgments, which will be surpassed by the bowls. For example, one-fourth of the human race dies in the fourth seal (Rev. 6:8), yet at a later time this increases to one-third dying in the sixth trumpet (Rev. 9:15).

The seals cover years (possibly two to two and a half years), the trumpets months (possibly twelve to eighteen months) and the bowls days (Dan. 12:11; Rev. 11:3; 12:6; 13:5). The time gap between the judgment events decreases as does the duration of the judgments themselves.

The seals alert us that something important is yet to come. The contents that are inside a scroll are always much more important than the seals that secure their privacy. The purpose of a seal is to keep private the contents inside the scroll. The seals are preparatory. They can be compared to the wrapping on a gift that must be removed to see what is inside the package. The trumpets warn us of something more severe to follow. They speak of an impending disaster that requires an extreme response to God. The bowls pour out in fullness without delay or hindrance.

Each series has seven events structured in a similar way, being divided into three parts with the first four events belonging together, the next two being clearly grouped together, and the final one standing alone. For example, the four horsemen form a group of four seals and are distinct from the remaining three seals. In the same way, the first four trumpets and bowls are distinct from the remaining three trumpets and bowls. As we understand this structure, we receive more insight into the judgment events.

SEVEN SEALS (Rev. 6:1-17; 8:1)			
1st Seal	White horse	Antichrist's political aggression	6:1-2
2nd Seal	Red horse	Bloodshed and final world war	6:3-4
3rd Seal	Black horse	Famine and economic crisis	6:5-6
4th Seal	Pale horse	One-fourth of humanity is killed	6:7-8
5th Seal	Prayer movement	Prayer is strengthened by martyrs	6:9-11
6th Seal	Cosmic disturbances	Cosmic disturbances and God's glory	6:12-17
7th Seal	Anointed prayer	Prayer is strengthened by the angels	8:1-6
SEVEN TRUMPETS (Rev. 8:2-9:21; 11:14-19)			
1st Trumpet	Food supply	One-third of the earth's vegetation is burned	8:7
2nd Trumpet	Food supply	One-third of the sea turns to blood	8:8-9
3rd Trumpet	Water supply	One-third of the fresh water becomes bitter	8:10-11
4th Trumpet	Light, energy	One-third of the sun, moon, and stars are darkened	8:12
5th Trumpet	Torment	Demonic locusts that torment for five months	9:1-12
6th Trumpet	Death	Demonic horsemen that kill one-third of the earth	9:13-21
7th Trumpet	Defeat	Seventh trumpet—the rapture and the return of Jesus (Rev. 11:15; 1 Cor. 15:52)	11:15-19
SEVEN BOWLS OF GOD'S WRATH (Rev. 15-16) i.e., plagues in Egypt (Ex. 7-12)			
1st Bowl	Sores	Loathsome sores on the Antichrist worshipers	16:2
2nd Bowl	Food supply	The sea turns to blood, killing all sea life	16:3
3rd Bowl	Water supply	The earth's fresh water turns to blood	16:4-7
4th Bowl	Torment	Men are scorched with great heat by the sun	16:8-9
5th Bowl	Destruction	Painful darkness on the Antichrist's empire	16:10-11
6th Bowl	Global guilt	Deceiving the nations to come to Armageddon	16:12-16
7th Bowl	Annihilation	Earthquake, hail and the final fall of Babylon	16:17-21

THE HARLOT BABYLON: THE ANTICHRIST'S TWO-STAGE STRATEGY

Revelation 17 gives us extraordinary insight into Satan's strategy to establish the harlot Babylon worldwide religion as a stepping stone to cause all the nations to worship the Antichrist. It vividly describes the seductive power and cruel persecution of the harlot Babylon's one-world, religious system.

The Antichrist has a two-fold strategy to cause all the nations to worship him. **Firstly**, he will use the harlot Babylon's religious "tolerance" to allure multitudes to take a step back from the allegiance they once had to the religious belief systems they grew up with. Satan knows that the leap will be too great for a nominal Christian, Jew, Muslim, or Hindu to suddenly leave their belief system to become a devoted worshiper of the Antichrist. At this time, many nominal Christians will fall away from the faith (1 Tim. 4:1; 2 Thes. 2:3).

Secondly, the Antichrist will replace Babylon's *tolerant* religion with his *intolerant* religion, characterized by a strict rigidity enforced with brutality (Rev. 13:4-18).

The harlot religion will serve as a "forerunner" to prepare the nations to worship the Antichrist. Thus, the harlot Babylon religion will be an essential step in the process to deceive the nations into worshiping the Antichrist. It will be a counterfeit "justice" movement that will masquerade as an answer to the ills of the world. It will allure multitudes by feeding the poor, meeting humanitarian needs, loving peace, and emphasizing the dignity of humanity. It will champion diversity and tolerance, and will have no moral absolutes.

The nations will rejoice as they drink from her golden cup and become intoxicated with her false promises of peace, compassion, and prosperity (Rev. 17:4). This religious system will boldly proclaim that no one religion is better than any other and that all roads lead to salvation. Finally, after she serves her purpose of weakening many people's allegiance to the belief systems of their personal religious heritage, the Antichrist, and the ten kings who work closely with him, will suddenly betray the harlot Babylon by destroying her (Rev. 17:16). This will occur in the middle of the final seven years of this age.

THE SECOND COMING AND THE RAPTURE

Paul teaches that the rapture will occur at the last trumpet (1 Cor. 15:52). It is the last in the series of seven numbered trumpets in Revelation (Rev. 8-9; 10:7; 11:15). At this time, the mystery of God or the plan of God for the Bride to be ready to rule the earth with Jesus will be complete (Rev. 10:7).

The Bible gives us three different descriptions of the rapture and events related to it at the last trumpet. They show us different facets of the one great diamond of Jesus' return.

Firstly, Jesus gives us a *cosmic view* of His coming by emphasizing His glory that will be seen in the sky; this is in Matthew 24:29-31.

Secondly, Paul gives us a *pastoral view* of Jesus' coming by emphasizing its effect on the saints—transforming our physical bodies and bringing us all together (1 Cor. 15:50-52; 1 Thes. 4-5).

Thirdly, John gives us a *political view* of Jesus' coming by emphasizing how His return will affect nations and impact world governments when He takes over all the kingdoms of this world (Rev. 11:15). John highlights the political view, since the theme of the book of Revelation is Jesus coming back to earth to reign as the King of kings over all nations (Rev. 1:7; 19:16). When Jesus comes back, He will replace all the evil governments on earth with His new government. This will be a hostile takeover, because the nations will be angry at Jesus and will resist His right to rule over them (Rev. 11:18; also Ps. 2:1-3).

Jesus' coming with all the saints involves a *royal procession* that has three stages, which will include many events occurring over a thirty-day period. The thirty-day period can be seen by comparing the *1,260 day* time frame (Dan. 7:25; 9:27; 12:7; Rev. 11:2-3; 12:6, 14; 13:5) with the *1,290 days* of Daniel 12:11. *See the article "Jesus' Thirty-Day Royal Procession" on page 116.*

- **Stage 1:** Jesus' royal procession across the sky to rapture the Church, during which He will be seen by every unbeliever in the earth (Mt. 24:30-31; Rev. 1:7). Every eye will see Him as His kingship is announced and asserted over each nation (Mt. 24:30; Rev. 1:7). Every person will see Him clearly enough to mourn—to have a deep emotional response. In other words, Jesus will travel close enough to the earth and slowly enough across the face of the earth for every unbeliever to see Him clearly enough to understand what is happening, so that they mourn over having not received Him.

- **Stage 2:** Jesus' royal procession on the land as He travels through Edom or modern-day Jordan (Isa. 63:1-6; Hab. 3:12; Ps. 110:5-6; 45:3-5).

- **Stage 3:** Jesus' triumphal entry to Jerusalem and the Mount of Olives, followed by His coronation (Ps. 24:7-10 ; Zech. 14:1-5; Rev. 19:11-21).

Summary: Jesus' royal procession will begin in the sky at the seventh trumpet (last trumpet; 1 Cor. 15:52; Rev. 11:15) with the rapture, and will end in Jerusalem with an astounding victory over the wicked armies that gather at Armageddon.

There will be three types of people on earth when Jesus appears in the sky:

- The *redeemed* will be raptured during Jesus' worldwide procession across the sky.
- The *reprobate,* who took the mark of the Beast, will be judged and then killed (some executed).
- The *resisters* are the unsaved survivors of the Great Tribulation, who will refuse to worship the Antichrist, even though they were not saved. Scripture refers to them as those who are left or those who remain (Isa. 4:3; 10:20; 11:11; 49:6; 65:8; 66:19; Jer. 31:2; Ezek. 20:38-42; 36:36; Dan. 12:1; Amos 9:9-10; Joel 2:32; Zech. 12:14; 13:8; 14:16). These will have an opportunity to be saved after Jesus returns to the earth. They are the ones who will populate the millennial earth.

JESUS' THIRTY-DAY ROYAL PROCESSION

Jesus' royal procession and the events that will dismantle the Antichrist's empire will cover a thirty-day period. An angel told Daniel about this thirty-day period that would extend beyond the commonly understood 1,260 days (three and a half years) in which most of God's end-time plan occurs (Dan. 12:11).

> *And from the time that the daily sacrifice is taken away, and the*
> *abomination of desolation is set up, there shall be 1,290 days.*
> *(Dan. 12:11)*

The Antichrist is the one who will set up the "abomination of desolation": he will stop the sacrifices in the temple in Jerusalem (which is soon to be rebuilt), cause an image of himself to stand in the holy place, and require everyone to worship him as God (Mt. 24:15; 2 Thes. 2:4; Rev. 13:14-18).

> *When you see the abomination of desolation spoken of by Daniel the*
> *prophet, standing in the holy place . . . then let those who are in Judea*
> *flee to the mountains. (Mt. 24:15-16)*

Thus, the Antichrist's worldwide worship system will be founded; it will be an abomination to God, resulting in the desolation of the nations by God's judgments, as seen in the Great Tribulation. The evil activities associated with the image of the Antichrist standing in the holy place of the Jerusalem temple will continue for exactly 1,290 days, which is thirty days *after* Jesus comes on the clouds in glory. Jesus will rapture the Church 1,260 days after the abomination of desolation is set up. Thus, what we learn from Daniel is that God will allow the Antichrist's worship system to function for thirty days *after* the Church is raptured at the seventh trumpet (Rev. 11:15).

All those who study end-time prophecy are familiar with the well-known three-and-a-half-year period that ends at the seventh trumpet. This three-and-a-half-year period is also referred to in Scripture as *42 months* or *1,260 days* (according to the Hebrew calendar). This same time frame is referred to as *time, times, and half a time*. *Time* refers to one year, *times* to two years, and *half a time* to half a year, making three and a half years.

This important 1,260-day period begins on the day the abomination of desolation is set up.

During these three and a half years, three activities pertaining to God's people will occur. They will all begin on the day the abomination of desolation begins, and they will continue for 1,260 days.

- Provision: God will make supernatural provision for the remnant of Israel for exactly 1,260 days (Rev. 12:6, 14).
- Prophecy: The two witnesses will prophesy for exactly 1,260 days (Rev. 11:3).
- Persecution: The Antichrist will war against the saints (Dan. 7:25; Rev. 13:5, 7) and dominate Jerusalem (Rev. 11:2; Dan. 12:7) for exactly 1,260 days.

Consequently, they will end on exactly the 1,260th day after the abomination of desolation begins. Why? This is the day the Church is raptured at the seventh trumpet (Rev. 11:15) and when the Antichrist's unchallenged domination of Jerusalem and Israel ends. His focus will change in a dramatic way on that day.

The question is: where will Jesus and the saints be during these thirty days? The three activities pertaining to God's people—provision, prophecy, and persecution—stop exactly 1,260 days after the abomination of desolation is set up, because that is when the saints are raptured: at the seventh trumpet.

At that time, Jesus will march up from Edom (Jordan, Isa. 63:1-6) to Israel as the greater Moses, releasing the bowl judgments on the Antichrist, a type of end-time Pharaoh. Jesus will march into Jerusalem to liberate Israel and kill the Antichrist and his armies, thus ending the abomination of desolation (Rev. 19:11-21).

Summary: this period of 1,260 days will end when Jesus comes in the sky at the seventh trumpet to rapture the saints (Rev. 11:15). The 1,290 days include an additional thirty days after the seventh trumpet, during which the Antichrist's worship system, or the abomination of desolation, continues on earth. It ends when Jesus marches into Jerusalem to personally destroy the Antichrist (2 Thes. 2:8; Rev. 19:20).

WHERE IS THE CHURCH IN THE BOOK OF REVELATION?

Some teach that the Church will be raptured before the Tribulation. This teaching is based on the argument that since the term *Church* is not mentioned after Revelation 4, the Church must no longer be on earth at that time. This is an assumption that is based on silence rather than what the Scripture directly says. There is much evidence in the book of Revelation that the saints will be living and functioning on earth during the Tribulation.

The great harvest of souls from all nations occurs during the Tribulation. The Church will not be absent at the time of her greatest increase and effectiveness in world evangelism.

> *Behold, a great multitude which no one could number, of all nations, tribes, peoples, and tongues, standing before the throne . . . These are the ones who come out of the great tribulation, and washed their robes and made them white in the blood of the Lamb. (Rev. 7:9, 14)*

The saints will overcome Satan and the Antichrist with great victory during the Tribulation.

> *They overcame him (Satan) by the blood of the Lamb and by the word of their testimony, and they did not love their lives to the death. (Rev. 12:11)*

Some of the saints will be martyred during the Tribulation. Therefore, the Church must be on earth for the saints to be killed during that time.

> *They have shed the blood of saints and prophets. (Rev. 16:6)*

> *I saw the woman (Babylon), drunk with the blood of the saints and with the blood of the martyrs of Jesus. (Rev. 17:6)*

> *In [Babylon] was found the blood of prophets and saints. (Rev. 18:24)*

> *He has avenged on [Babylon] the blood of His servants shed by her. (Rev. 19:2)*

> *"How long . . . until You judge and avenge our blood on those who dwell on the earth?" . . . they should rest a little while longer, until both the number of their fellow servants and their brethren, who would be killed as they were, was completed. (Rev. 6:10–11)*

I saw the souls of those who had been beheaded for their witness to Jesus and for the word of God, who had not worshiped the beast (Antichrist). (Rev. 20:4)

The saints must be on earth during the Tribulation for the Antichrist to war against them.

It was granted to him (Antichrist) to make war with the saints. (Rev. 13:7)

The dragon (Satan) was enraged with the woman, and he went to make war with the rest of her offspring, who keep the commandments of God and have the testimony of Jesus Christ. (Rev. 12:17)

The prayers of the saints during the Tribulation will release the trumpet judgments. The prayers of "all" the saints include both the accumulated prayers through history as well as the accelerated prayers in the generation the Lord returns.

Another angel . . . was given much incense, that he should offer it with the prayers of all the saints . . . The smoke of the incense, with the prayers of the saints, ascended before God from the angel's hand. Then the angel took the censer, filled it with fire from the altar, and threw it to the earth. (Rev. 8:3-5)

Jesus will return in answer to the prayer of the saints on the earth crying out for His return.

The Spirit and the Bride say, "Come!" (Rev. 22:17)

Prophetic ministry will increase greatly in the saints who will be on earth during the Tribulation (Dan. 11:33–35; 12:10; Joel 2:28–32; Acts 2:17–21; Eph. 4:13; Rev. 11:3–6, 10, 18; 16:6; 18:20, 24; 22:6–9). The seven thunders prophecies were sealed in John's generation (Rev. 10:4). The clear implication here is that God will release them during the Tribulation to the end-time prophets.

The two witnesses or prophets will be born-again believers.

I will give power to My two witnesses, and they will prophesy 1,260 days. (Rev. 11:3)

Calculating the number of the Antichrist will be relevant to those living in the Tribulation who study the Scripture and believe it. In other words, this is written for the aid of believers.

> *Here is wisdom. Let him who has understanding calculate the number of the beast, for it is the number of a man: His number is 666. (Rev. 13:18)*

An angel commanded God's people to leave Babylon just prior to her final judgment in Revelation 18. For this command to be relevant, the saints, as the only group who will actively obey the commands of God, must be on the earth.

> *I heard another voice from heaven saying, "Come out of her, My people, lest you share in her sins, and lest you receive of her plagues." (Rev. 18:4)*

Only those on earth during the events prophesied by John will be in a position to keep the prophecy to the full degree. Believers through history have kept the prophecy in the sense of obeying the commands that Jesus gave in the prophecy, such as abstaining from immorality (Rev. 2:14, 20). Keeping the prophecy in its full sense means to participate with Jesus in the unfolding of the holy drama described in the prophecy itself.

> *Behold, I am coming quickly! Blessed is he who keeps the words of the prophecy of this book. (Rev. 22:7)*

An angel revealed to Daniel that the saints would be purified and made wise during the pressures of the Tribulation described in Daniel 12.

> *Many shall be purified, made white, and refined, but the wicked shall do wickedly . . . but the wise shall understand. (Dan. 12:10)*

THE ROLE OF PRAYER IN REVELATION AND THE END-TIME CHURCH

In Revelation 8:1-6, John saw an open vision of an angel working together with the prayers of all the saints in a way that resulted in God's fire or the trumpet judgments being released to the earth in the end times. The saints are only to pray for these judgments after the Tribulation begins, and only on the reprobate who take the mark of the Beast (signifying their final rejection of the gospel and their oppression of the saints). The prayers of "all" the saints are both those that are accumulated from history as well as those accelerated in the generation in which the Lord returns.

> *Another angel . . . was given much incense, that he should offer it with the prayers of all the saints . . . The smoke of the incense, with the prayers of the saints, ascended before God . . . Then the angel took the censer, filled it with fire . . . and threw it to the earth. (Rev. 8:3-5)*

David prophesied about a generation whose praise songs of intercession resulted in releasing God's written judgments or His vengeance on the wickedness in the nations. David presented this authority in prayer as being an honor that God has given all the saints. The fullness of this will be seen in the end times.

> *Let the high praises of God be in their mouth . . . to execute vengeance on the nations, and punishments on the peoples; to bind their kings with chains . . . To execute on them the written judgment—This honor have all His saints! (Ps. 149:6–9)*

Jesus prophesied of a time when God's people would cry out night and day to release His judgments against oppression. This will find its greatest expression in the generation in which the Son of Man comes.

> *And shall God not avenge His own elect who cry out day and night to Him . . .? I tell you that He will avenge them speedily . . . when the Son of Man comes, will He really find faith on the earth . . .? (Lk. 18:7–8)*

The prayers of the martyrs in heaven will also be used to release God's end-time judgments.

They cried with a loud voice, saying, "How long, O Lord, holy and true, until You judge and avenge our blood on those who dwell on the earth?" (Rev. 6:10)

The psalmist described a people who would live in a future generation. They were not yet created or born at the time in which this psalm was written. He prophesied of the Lord answering their prayer. Some were destitute because they were facing martyrdom.

He shall regard the prayer of the destitute, and shall not despise their prayer. This will be written for the generation to come, that a people yet to be created may praise the LORD. For He looked down . . . from heaven the LORD viewed the earth, to hear the groaning of the prisoner, to release those appointed to death. (Ps. 102:17–20)

Jesus' second coming will be in answer to unceasing prayer that cries out for Him to come. This will be fulfilled in the hour of history when the Church across the nations sees herself as His Bride. There has never been a time in history when the Church, with a bridal identity, universally prayed for His return. This cry for His return in the context of revelation of Jesus as the Bridegroom God is beginning to emerge in the Church across the nations in this very hour.

The Spirit and the Bride say, "Come!" (Rev. 22:17)

Jesus will not release the end-time seal judgments until the bowls of prayer around the throne are full. This speaks of the priority and maturity of the Church's prayer ministry before the end-time seal judgments are released.

When He had taken the scroll . . . the twenty-four elders fell down before the Lamb, each having a harp, and golden bowls full of incense, which are the prayers of the saints. (Rev. 5:8)

Each reference in the book of Revelation to the heavenly altar around God's throne gives us insight into the end-time prayer ministry. The heavenly altar is the place in heaven where our prayers ascend to the throne. Thus, when a judgment decree is given from the heavenly altar, it is to be understood as being released in response to prayer.

The sixth angel sounded: I heard a voice from the four horns of the golden altar. (Rev. 9:13)

Another angel came out from the altar . . . and he cried with a loud cry to him who had the sharp sickle, saying, "Thrust in your sharp sickle . . . for her grapes are fully ripe." (Rev. 14:18)

I heard another from the altar saying, "Even so, Lord God Almighty, true and righteous are Your judgments." (Rev. 16:7)

Isaiah prophesied of a generation that would continue in day and night prayer until Jerusalem was established as a praise in all the earth. This will not happen until the time of Jesus' second coming. In this passage, Isaiah spoke of 24/7 prayer ministries that would not be silent until Jesus made Jerusalem the chief city in the earth at the time of His coming.

I have set watchmen (intercessors) on your walls, O Jerusalem; who shall never hold their peace day or night. You who make mention of the LORD, do not keep silent, and give Him no rest till He establishes and till He makes Jerusalem a praise in the earth. (Isa. 62:6–7)

Shall God not avenge His own elect who cry out day and night to Him? (Lk. 18:7)

Isaiah prophesied of the generation that would worship and pray from the ends of the earth until the second coming of Jesus as a mighty man of war to prevail against the Antichrist.

Sing to the LORD a new song, and His praise from the ends of the earth . . . Let the wilderness and its cities lift up their voice . . . let them shout from the top of the mountains. Let them give glory to the LORD, and declare His praise in the coastlands. The LORD shall go forth like a mighty man; He shall stir up His zeal like a man of war. He shall cry out, yes, shout aloud; He shall prevail against His enemies. I have held My peace a long time, I have been still and restrained Myself. Now I will cry like a woman in labor, I will pant and gasp at once. I will lay waste the mountains and hills. (Isa. 42:10–15)

In Isaiah 30, Isaiah was prophesying about the generation in which the Lord returns. He taught that the Lord waits until He hears the prayer of His people before He answers with great grace.

> *The LORD will wait, that He may be gracious to you . . . that He may have mercy on you . . . For the people shall dwell in Zion at Jerusalem; you shall weep no more. He will be very gracious to you at the sound of your cry; when He hears it, He will answer you. (Isa. 30:18–19)*

Isaiah recorded the prayer that many in Israel will pray just before Jesus returns. They will cry out for the Messiah to come and make His name known to the Antichrist and his nations who will be God's adversaries. Jesus will fully answer this prayer as He rends the heaven to come back to earth. At that time the nations will tremble before God. This prayer will be prayed especially by Messianic believers who confess Israel's sin with identificational repentance (Isa. 64:5-13).

> *Oh, that You would rend the heavens! that You would come down! That the mountains might shake at Your presence . . . to make Your name known to Your adversaries, that the nations may tremble at Your presence. (Isa. 64:1–2)*

Isaiah prophesied about the prayer ministry in Egypt in the generation in which the Lord returns. They will cry out because of the oppression of the Antichrist. God will answer them by sending Jesus to them as their savior.

> *It will be for a sign and for a witness to the LORD of hosts in the land of Egypt; for they will cry to the LORD because of the oppressors, and He will send them a Savior and a Mighty One, and He will deliver them . . . they will return to the LORD, and He will be entreated by them and heal them. (Isa. 19:20–22)*

Isaiah prophesied many times about the role of prayer in the generation in which the Lord returns. Each of the passages below describes the generation in which the Lord returns.

> *They shall lift up their voice, they shall sing; for the majesty of the LORD they shall cry aloud from the sea. Therefore glorify the LORD . . . in the coastlands of the sea. From the ends of the earth we have heard songs: "Glory to the righteous!" (Isa. 24:14–16)*

It will be said in that day: "Behold, this is our God; we have waited (prayed) for Him . . . This is the LORD; we have waited for Him . . . and rejoice in His salvation." (Isa. 25:9)

In the way of Your judgments, O LORD, we have waited (prayed) for You. . . For when Your judgments are in the earth, the inhabitants of the world will learn righteousness. (Isa. 26:8–9)

Put Me in remembrance; let us contend together (prayer); state your case. (Isa. 43:26)

Your watchmen (intercessors) shall lift up their voices, with their voices they shall sing together; for they shall see eye to eye when the LORD brings back Zion. (Isa. 52:8)

Jeremiah prophesied about the role of prayer in the generation in which Jesus will return.

Sing with gladness for Jacob, and shout among the chief of the nations; proclaim, give praise, and say, "O LORD, save Your people, the remnant of Israel!'"(Jer. 31:7)

Zechariah prophesied often about the place of prayer in the time frame related to Jesus' return.

The inhabitants of one city shall go to another, saying, "Let us continue to go and pray before the LORD . . . " Yes, many peoples and strong nations shall come to seek the LORD of hosts in Jerusalem, and to pray before the LORD. (Zech. 8:21–22)

Ask the LORD for rain in the time of the latter rain. The LORD will make flashing clouds . . . (Zech. 10:1)

I will pour on the house of David . . . the Spirit of grace and supplication. (Zech. 12:10)

I will bring the one-third through the fire, will refine them as silver is refined . . . they will call on My name, and I will answer them. I will say, "This is My people." (Zech. 13:9)

THE MILLENNIUM: HEAVEN ON EARTH

The Millennium is a 1,000-year period in which Jesus will rule the world in righteousness. The word millennium is from the Latin *mille*, which means "a thousand." Thus, it is common to refer to this future 1,000-year earthly reign of Jesus as the Millennium. At this time the kingdom of God will be openly manifest worldwide, affecting every sphere of life (politics, agriculture, economics, education, family, media, arts, technology, environment, social institutions, etc.).

> *I saw thrones, and they (saints) sat on them . . . They lived and reigned with Christ for a thousand years . . . They shall reign with Him a thousand years. (Rev. 20:4-6)*

This period of blessing will be initiated by Jesus' second coming. The result will be a 1,000-year period of unprecedented blessing for the whole earth as Jesus establishes righteousness and prosperity, and restores the agriculture, atmosphere, and animal life to the conditions that were seen in the garden of Eden (Deut. 8; 28; Isa. 2:1-4; 9:6-9; 11:1-16; 51:1-8; 60-62; 65:17-25; Ps. 2:6-12; 110:1-7; Mt. 5:5; 6:10; 17:11; 19:28; 28:19; Acts 1:6; 3:21; Rev. 20:1-6).

> *Your kingdom come. Your will be done on earth as it is in heaven. (Mt. 6:10)*

Jesus, as King of kings, will personally govern a worldwide kingdom from Jerusalem. All the kings of the earth will be saved, will worship Jesus, and will base their national governments on His Word (Ps. 72:11; 102:15; 138:4; 148:11; Isa. 62:2; Rev. 21:24).

> *Jerusalem shall be called the Throne of the LORD, and all the nations shall be gathered to it, to the name of the LORD, to Jerusalem. (Jer. 3:17)*

Jesus will rule the millennial earth that has natural and supernatural dimensions. For example, the length of life will be extended as it was in Noah's time and the animosity between animals and humans will be removed. Those who live to be only 100 years old will be thought to have lived a short life. It will be common for people to live to be 500 years old.

No more shall an infant from there live but a few days, nor an old man who has not fulfilled his days; for the child shall die one hundred years old, but the sinner being one hundred years old shall be accursed. They shall build houses and inhabit them; they shall plant vineyards and eat their fruit . . . For as the days of a tree, so shall be the days of My people . . . The wolf and the lamb shall feed together, the lion shall eat straw like the ox. (Isa. 65:20-25)

The wolf also shall dwell with the lamb . . . the calf and the young lion and the fatling together; and a little child shall lead them. The cow and the bear shall graze; their young ones shall lie down together; and the lion shall eat straw like the ox. The nursing child shall play by the cobra's hole . . . They shall not hurt nor destroy in all My holy mountain, for the earth shall be full of the knowledge of the LORD as the waters cover the sea. (Isa. 11:6-9)

The natural processes of life will continue. There will be a need for social infrastructures to provide for the necessities of life (food, water, and electricity), building projects (buildings, highways, and bridges), economic systems (currencies, banking, and investments), spiritual life (worship centers, Bible schools, and churches), education (from elementary to university), agriculture (equipment and distribution), media and arts, technology, and environmental and social institutions. Cities that were destroyed in the Tribulation will be restored (Isa. 62:8-9; 65:21-23; Jer. 31:5; Ezek. 48:18-19). Justice will be established over every sphere of life (Isa. 9:7; 11:3-5; 10:22; 28:17; 32:16; 42:1-4).

The centerpiece of God's eternal purpose is for Jesus to come back to establish His kingdom over all the earth as He joins the heavenly and earthly realms together. God created the universe in two distinct realms. Heaven speaks of the spiritual realm where God's power and presence are openly manifest. Earth speaks of the physical realm where human process, emotions, and physical sensation reach their fullest expression.

Having made known to us the mystery (hidden plan) of His will . . . that He might gather together in one ALL things in Christ, both which are in heaven and which are on earth—in Him. (Eph. 1:9-10)

EXTENDED OUTLINE OF THE BOOK OF REVELATION

PT 1: JOHN'S CALLING TO PROPHESY (REV. 1)
- Introduction and greeting (1:1-6)
- Announcement of Jesus' second coming (1:7)
- The Lord's self-designation (1:8)
- John's calling to prophesy about the end times (1:9-20)

PT 2: JESUS' SEVEN LETTERS TO THE SEVEN CHURCHES (REV. 2-3)
- **Ephesus**: return to wholehearted love for Jesus (2:1-7)
- **Smyrna**: continue to stand strong without fear in persecution (2:8-11)
- **Pergamos**: repent of compromise with immorality and idolatry (2:12-17)
- **Thyatira**: repent of compromise with immorality and idolatry (2:18-29)
- **Sardis**: repent of spiritual deadness (3:1-6)
- **Philadelphia**: continue to stand strong in faithfulness (3:7-13)
- **Laodicea**: repent of spiritual lukewarmness (3:14-22)

PT 3: JESUS TAKES THE SCROLL (REV. 4-5)
- The Father seated on the throne (4:1-11)
- Jesus takes the scroll: contains the earth's title deed and plan to cleanse the earth (5:1-14)

PT 4: JESUS' BATTLE PLAN: FIVE CHRONOLOGICAL SECTIONS (REV. 6-22)
CHRONOLOGICAL SECTION #1: SEAL JUDGMENTS (REV. 6)
- 1st seal: white horse—Antichrist's political aggression (6:1-2)
- 2nd seal: red horse—bloodshed and final world war (6:3-4)
- 3rd seal: black horse—famine and economic crisis (6:5-6)
- 4th sea: pale horse—one-fourth of humanity is killed (6:7-8)
- 5th seal: prayer is strengthened by the martyrs (6:9-11)
- 6th seal: cosmic disturbances and God's glory (6:12-17

ANGELIC EXPLANATION #1: PROTECTION (REV. 7)
- Sealing of the 144,000 on earth (7:1-8)
- Great worldwide harvest (7:9-17)

CHRONOLOGICAL SECTION #2: TRUMPET JUDGMENTS (REV. 8-9)
- 7th seal: prayer is strengthened by the angels (8:1-6)
- 1st trumpet: one-third of the earth's vegetation is burned (8:7)
- 2nd trumpet: one-third of the sea turns to blood (8:8-9)
- 3rd trumpet: one-third of the fresh water becomes bitter (8:10-11)
- 4th trumpet: one-third of the sun, moon, and stars are darkened (8:12)
- 5th trumpet: demonic locusts that torment for five months (9:1-12)
- 6th trumpet: demonic horsemen that kill one-third of the earth (9:13-21)

ANGELIC EXPLANATION #2: DIRECTION (REV. 10:1-11:13)
- The seven thunders prophetic messages and John's little book (10:1-11)
- The two witnesses (11:1-13)

CHRONOLOGICAL SECTION #3: 2ND COMING PROCESSION (REV. 11:14-19)
- 7th trumpet: the rapture and the return of Jesus
- At the seventh trumpet, the Church is raptured and a heavenly announcement is made that Jesus will replace all the governments of the earth. At this time, the saints will be rewarded and the wicked people on earth will be destroyed.

ANGELIC EXPLANATION #3: VIOLENT CONFRONTATION (REV. 12-14)
- Woman (Israel) with the male Child (Jesus) is persecuted (12:1-17)
- Antichrist: his head wound and support by ten kings (13:1-10)
- False Prophet: image of Beast/mark of Beast (13:11-18)
- Jesus with the 144,000 on Mount Zion (14:1-5)
- Four angelic messages: essential prophetic themes to proclaim (14:6-13)
- Two harvests: righteous (14:14-16) and unrighteous (14:17-20)

CHRONOLOGICAL SECTION #4: BOWL JUDGMENTS (REV. 15-16)

- Heavenly scene—seven angels with seven bowls of wrath (Rev. 15)
- 1st bowl: loathsome sores on the Antichrist worshipers (16:1-2)
- 2nd bowl: the sea turns to blood, killing all sea life (16:3)
- 3rd bowl: the earth's fresh water turns to blood (16:4-7)
- 4th bowl: men are scorched with great heat by the sun (16:8-9)
- 5th bowl: painful darkness on the Antichrist's empire (16:10-11)
- 6th bowl: deceiving the nations to come to Armageddon (16:12-16)
- 7th bowl: earthquake, hail, and the final fall of Babylon (16:17-21)

ANGELIC EXPLANATION #4: SEDUCTION BABYLON (REV. 17:1-19:10)

- The great harlot's seduction of the nations (17:1-6)
- The mystery of the woman and Beast (17:7-18)
- The fall of Babylon (18:1-24)
- Heaven praises the Father for judging Babylon (19:1-5)
- The marriage supper of the Lamb (19:6-10)

CHRONOLOGICAL SECTION #5: TRIUMPHAL ENTRY (REV. 19:11-21:8)

- Jesus marches through the land on His way to Jerusalem (19:11-16)
- Jesus defeats the Antichrist and False Prophet at Jerusalem (19:17-21)
- Millennial kingdom: 1,000-year reign of Jesus and the saints (20:1-10)
- The saints reign with Christ for 1,000 years (20:4-6)
- Satan released to deceive the nations, but defeated once for all (20:7-10)
- The great white throne judgment of all unbelievers (20:11-15)

ANGELIC EXPLANATION #5: RESTORATION (REV. 21:9-22:5)

- Jerusalem described: external view seen as the Holy of Holies (21:9-21)
- Jerusalem described: internal view seen as garden of Eden (21:22-22:5)

FINAL EXHORTATION (REV. 22:6-21)

- The time is near, do not seal up the book (22:6-11)
- The Spirit and the Bride cry out for His return (22:12-17)
- Warning to not tamper with the Book (22:18-21)

THE SEVEN MAIN SYMBOLS OF THE BOOK OF REVELATION

All the events and numbers in Revelation are to be taken in their plain, literal meaning unless specifically indicated otherwise (Rev. 1:20; 5:6; 11:8; 12:1, 3, 9; 17:7, 9, 15-18, etc). The seven main symbols in Revelation are all in chapters 12-14. Daniel used most of these symbols (Dan. 7:3-7, 12, 17; 8:4). He prophesied of the Antichrist as the Beast with a vast empire (Dan. 7:7, 11, 19-23) that was supported by ten kings who he spoke of as ten horns on the Antichrist (Dan. 7:7, 2:41-42 ; 20, 24; Rev. 12:3; 13:1; 17:3, 7, 12, 16).

The dragon: always symbolic of Satan (Rev. 12:3, 4, 7, 9, 13, 16, 17; 13:2, 4; 16:13; 20:2).

The first beast: is symbolic of the Antichrist (Rev. 13; 14:9-11; 17:3-17; 19:19-21; 20:4, 10). Daniel prophesied of the Antichrist as the Beast with a vast empire (Dan. 7:7, 11, 19-23).

Another beast: is symbolic of the False Prophet, who is only called *another beast* once. Every other time he is referred to as the False Prophet (Rev. 13:11-17; 16:13; 19:20; 20:10).

The seven heads: the seven historical empires that persecuted Israel are Egypt, Assyria, Babylon, Persia, Greece, ancient Rome, and a still-future, revived Roman Empire (Dan. 2:41-42; 7:7, 20, 24; Rev. 12:3; 13:1; 17:3-16).

The ten horns: speak of a future ten-nation confederation of ten kings who rule simultaneously over their own nations as they come into an enthusiastic agreement or partnership together under the Antichrist's authority (Dan. 2:41-42; 7:7, 20, 24; 11:36-45; Rev. 12:3; 13:1; 17:3, 7, 12, 16). Daniel prophesied of the Antichrist as the Beast with a vast empire (Dan. 7:7, 11, 19-23) that was supported by ten kings whom he spoke of as ten horns on the Antichrist (Dan. 2:41-42; 7:7, 20, 24; 11:36-45; Rev. 12:3; 13:1; 17:3, 7, 12, 16).

The harlot Babylon: will be established in the literal, rebuilt city of Babylon on the Euphrates River in Iraq (fifty miles south of Baghdad) that will be restored and used as a headquarters for the Antichrist. It will function as the center of worldwide, demonic, religious and economic networks (Isa. 13-14; 21; Jer. 50-51; Rev. 17-18). It will seduce many to sin and will persecute the saints.

The woman with the male Child (Jesus): the woman is the faithful remnant of Israel throughout history (Rev. 12:1-5) who gives birth to the male Child, who is Jesus. Satan wars with her offspring, who are Gentile believers (Rev. 12:17).

GLOSSARY

abomination of desolation: The Antichrist will claim to be God and demand to be worshiped (Rev. 13). This will be the abomination that leads to great desolation. God's judgments will bring desolation, or destruction, to all who participate in this terrible abomination (Dan. 9:27; Mt. 24:15; Mk. 13:14; 2 Thes. 2:3-4). This worship system will be based on the Antichrist (called the Beast) setting up an image (statue or idol) of himself in the Jerusalem temple. This image will be demonically empowered to breathe and speak (Rev. 13:14-15). No one will be able to buy or sell without worshiping the Antichrist before this image (Rev. 13:16-18). All who refuse will be sought out as criminals of the state under a threat of martyrdom.

The image of the Beast is one of the most significant prophetic signs in the end times. John emphasized it ten times (Rev. 13:14, 15 [3x]; 14:9, 11; 15:2; 16:2; 19:20; 20:4). The mark of the Beast will provide economic support for the Antichrist's worship movement and will penalize those who resist.

The abomination of desolation is described nine times (Dan. 8:13; 9:26, 27; 11:31; 12:11; Mt. 24:15; Mk. 13:14; 2 Thes. 2:3-4; Rev. 13:12-18). The image of the Beast and the mark of the Beast will be two components of the abomination of desolation system that will mobilize and finance the Antichrist's global worship movement (Rev. 13:13-18). The image of the Beast will mobilize Antichrist's worshipers and penalize those who resist.

advent: Derived from the Latin word *adventus*, which means arrival or coming. It is used to speak of both Jesus' first coming and second coming as the first and the second advents.

angelic explanations: This is the phrase we use for the five sections in the structure of the book of Revelation that function as a parenthesis, when the main story line of the book in the chronological sections is put "on pause." In these passages, an angel answers questions that arise from the chronological sections such as: Why is God's wrath so severe? What will happen to us? Angels explain to John what happens to God's people, including what Jesus will do to help us and what the Antichrist will do to persecute us. The five angelic explanations are found in the following passages: Revelation 7:1-17; 10:1-11:14; 12:1-14:20; 17:1-19:10; 21:9-22:5.

Antichrist: The word *anti* means against or in place of. The Antichrist is a demonized man who will be against Christ and will seek to be worshiped by the nations in place of Jesus. He will lead the most powerful and most wicked worldwide empire in history.

Summary of the Antichrist—the most powerful, evil, political leader in history		
Military genius	Tactics/strategy	Rev. 6:2; 13:2,16; Dan. 8:24, 25; 11:38-39
Oratorical genius	Moves masses of people	Dan. 11:32, 36; 8:23
Political genius	Diplomacy	Rev. 13:8, 12; 2 Thes. 2:4; Dan. 7:23
Commercial genius	Prosperity	Dan. 11:36, 43; 8:24; Rev. 13:16-17
Intellectual genius	Science, math, technology	Dan. 8:23; 7:25
Occult genius	Demonology, miracles	Dan. 8:24; 11:39; Rev. 13

another beast: A name for the False Prophet (Rev. 13:11).

apocalypse: Means unveiling or revealing and is translated as *revelation*. It is another name for the book of Revelation because it unveils or reveals the glory of Jesus and His end-time battle plan to drive evil off the planet.

apostasy: A falling away or departure from the Christian faith (Mt. 24:9-13; 2 Thes. 2:3; 1 Tim. 4:1-2; 2 Tim. 3:1-7; 4:3-4; 2 Pet. 2:1-3). An apostate is one who has fallen away from the Christian faith.

Armageddon campaign: A great military campaign that will continue for the final three and a half years in the land of Israel before Jesus returns. It will end with the battle of Jerusalem (Zech. 12:3; 14:1-2). The place the nations gather is called, in Hebrew, Armageddon (Rev. 16:16). The word *Armageddon* is from the Greek rendering of the Hebrew name *Har Megiddo*, which means "the hill of Megiddo" (*har* means "hill"). Megiddo is an ancient town in the valley of Jezreel, also called the valley of Esdraelon in the Plain of Jezreel. The plain of Megiddo, on which the hill of Megiddo stands, is the military staging area for this campaign in northern Israel.

Babylon: Historically, the chief city of the Babylonian empire, which was in the lower valley of the Tigris and Euphrates rivers in what is modern-day Iraq. This refers to the literal city of Babylon in Iraq (fifty miles south of Baghdad) that will be rebuilt and used as one of the headquarters of the Antichrist. It will function as the center of worldwide, demonic, religious and economic networks (Rev. 17-18). As

Jerusalem suddenly came out of the ashes and was rebuilt, so Babylon (in Iraq) will be suddenly rebuilt. Many of the specific details in the judgments prophesied about Babylon's sudden and permanent destruction in Jeremiah chapters 50 and 51 and Isaiah chapters 13, 14, and 21 have not yet fully happened. They were only partially fulfilled in history.

Beast: Term used thirty-six times to refer to the Antichrist (Rev. 13; 14:9-11; 17:3-17; 19:19-21; 20:4, 10).

canonized: Literature approved as part of the Holy Scripture or the biblical canon. The sixty-six books in the Bible are the only books that we accept as being canonized. The book of Revelation is a canonized prayer manual because it is divinely inspired and infallible. Therefore, it will bring unity to the end-time prayer movement.

chronological sections: The phrase we use for the five sections in the structure of the book of Revelation that describe the judgment events occurring on earth in God's end-time plan. They include the twenty-one judgment events (seven seals, seven trumpets, and seven bowls) that will happen on earth in chronological order during the Great Tribulation and the millennial kingdom. The five chronological sections are found in the following passages: Revelation chapter 6; chapters 8-9; 11:15-19; chapters 15-16, and 19:11-21:8.

Daniel's Seventieth Week: The final seven-year period before Jesus' second coming is referred to as Daniel's seventieth week. Daniel prophesied of seventy weeks (Dan. 9:24-27). Each "week" speaks of a period of seven years (instead of seven days). Jacob spoke of seven years as a "week" of years (Gen. 29:27-28). Seventy weeks of seven years totals 490 years. This prophecy concerns God's prophetic time calendar in dealing with the salvation of the nation of Israel. The seventy weeks (each week is seven years) concern God's plan for Israel from the days of Daniel to Jesus' second coming. The first sixty-nine weeks (483 years) are from 445 BC to the time of Christ's triumphal entry into Jerusalem (30 AD). The last week is a seven-year period that will not be fulfilled until Jesus' second coming. It will be initiated when Israel signs a peace treaty with the Antichrist, who is called "the prince who is to come" from a still-future, revived Roman Empire (Dan. 9:26-27).

Daniel's thirty-day period: Jesus' royal procession, along with the transitional events that will dismantle the Antichrist's empire, will cover a thirty-day period. In Daniel 12:11, an angel told Daniel about a thirty-day period that would extend beyond the commonly understood 1,260 days (three and a half years) in which

God makes supernatural provision for the remnant of Israel (Rev. 12:6, 14), the two witnesses prophesy (Rev. 11:3), and the Antichrist persecutes the Church and Israel by making war on the saints (Dan. 7:25; Rev. 13:5, 7) and dominating Jerusalem (Rev. 11:2; Dan. 12:7). This period of 1,260 days ends when Jesus comes in the sky at the seventh trumpet to rapture the saints (Rev. 11:17). The 1,290 days speak of an additional thirty days after the seventh trumpet in which the Antichrist's worship system or the abomination of desolation continues on earth. It ends when Jesus marches into Jerusalem to personally destroy the Antichrist (2 Thes. 2:8; Rev. 19:20).

dragon: Symbolic of Satan (Rev. 12:3, 4, 7, 9, 13, 16, 17; 13:2, 4; 16:13; 20:2).

eschatology: A term that speaks of the study of the end times. The word eschatology is made up of two different Greek words: *eschaton*, meaning end, and -*ology*, meaning a study of something. The most important events predicted in the end of the age (the *eschaton*) are the Great Tribulation, Jesus' second coming, and the millennial kingdom. More than one-fourth of the Scriptures (27%) relate to events foretold by the prophets.

False Prophet: The Antichrist's "minister of propaganda," who will work miracles (Rev. 16:13; 19:20; 20:10). He is called "another beast" in Revelation 13:11.

great white throne judgment: The time at the end of the Millennium, when all unbelievers will be judged by God and thrown into the lake of fire (Rev. 20:11-15).

harlot Babylon: The worldwide, demonically-inspired, religious and economic system based in the rebuilt city of Babylon, Iraq (Jer. 50-51; Rev. 17-18). See **Babylon**.

hermeneutics: The study of the interpretation of Scripture.

image of the Beast: A statue or idol of the Antichrist that will be set up in the Jerusalem temple. This image will be demonically empowered so that it will seem to think, talk, breathe, and make laws (Rev. 13:14-16). The main idol will be set up in the Jerusalem temple. It may be connected to a global network of idols. The image will be a significant, prophetic sign in the end times. John emphasized this image ten times (Rev. 13:14, 15 [3x]; 14:9, 11; 15:2; 16:2; 19:20; 20:4).

Jesus' end-time battle plan: This is a phrase we use to refer to Jesus' plan to raise up a praying Church to release the seal, trumpet, and bowl judgments (Rev. 6-22) to destroy the Antichrist and the False Prophet and those who follow them.

judgment seat of Christ: The time when Jesus evaluates the life of all true believers, resulting in some receiving rewards and others suffering loss of rewards (1 Cor. 3:10-15; 2 Cor. 5:10; Rom. 14:10-12). This evaluation occurs immediately after the Church has been raptured at the seventh trumpet (Rev. 11:18).

lake of fire: The final place of judgment for the Antichrist, False Prophet, Satan, demons, and all unbelievers (Rev. 20:15). Unbelievers will take part in the resurrection of condemnation, enduring eternal torment of body and soul (Jn. 5:29).

little horn: A term used by Daniel that refers to the Antichrist (Dan 7:7-8; 19, 25).

mark of the Beast: Will most likely be a form of technology, like a microchip implant, that the Antichrist will require everyone to have in order to buy or sell during the last three and a half years of the Tribulation (Rev. 13:16-18).

marriage supper of the Lamb: A time after the rapture when Jesus celebrates His wedding to the redeemed as His Bride (Rev. 19:7-10). Some believe that it will last the entire 1,000 years of the millennial kingdom.

Messiah: Comes from the Hebrew word *meshiach*, meaning "anointed one." It is translated as the Greek word *Christos* and the English word *Christ*. In the Old Testament, the Messiah was the coming anointed one who was to be king of Israel and lead the Jewish people to freedom from Gentile oppression.

Millennium: The Millennium is a literal 1,000-year period, in which Jesus will rule the whole world from Jerusalem in righteousness and peace. The kingdom of God will be openly manifest worldwide, affecting every sphere of life (politics, society, agriculture, economics, education, family, media, arts, environment, social institutions, etc).

New Jerusalem: The heavenly city where all the saints will live forever in God's immediate presence (Heb. 11:10, 16; 12:22-24). The New Jerusalem will descend to the earth in two stages: first, at the time of Jesus' second coming (Rev. 21:10) and then after the millennial kingdom (Rev. 21:2).

new heaven and earth: Names that are used in Scripture in two different contexts, both the Millennium and the eternal state (Isa. 65:17-25; 66:22-24; 2 Pet. 3:13; Rev. 21:1-2). The earth will continue forever (1 Chr. 23:25; 28:8; Ps. 37:29; 78:69; 104:5; 105:10-11; 125:1-2; Isa. 60:21; Ezek. 37:25; Joel 3:20).

Olivet Discourse: Jesus' main prophecy on the end times (Mt. 24; Mk. 13; Lk. 21).

parousia: A Greek word that means presence or coming of an important person. *Parousia* is the word that is used for Jesus' second "coming" (Mt. 24:3, 27, 37, 39; 1 Thes. 3:13; 4:15; 5:23; 2 Thes. 2:1, 8; Jas. 5:7-8).

posttribulation rapture (posttrib.): The word *post* means "after." This refers to the biblical teaching that the rapture and the second coming occur "after" the Tribulation. In other words, the Church will be on earth, walking in victory through the Tribulation. This will be the Church's finest hour, when the power of God will be experienced in great measure, surpassing any other time in history.

pretribulation rapture (pretrib.): The word *pre* means "before." This refers to an unbiblical teaching that says the rapture occurs "before" the Tribulation. This popular teaching claims that Christians will not go through the Tribulation. It is based partially on a wrong view of the Tribulation as a time when the saints come under God's judgments. The Bible is clear that the saints are not ordained to receive God's wrath (Rom. 5:9; 1 Thes. 5:9)

rapture: It comes from the Latin word *raptus*, which means "catching away." The saints who are alive on earth when Jesus returns will be caught away to meet the Lord in the air (1 Thes. 4:17). The rapture occurs at the time of the seventh trumpet, which is the last trumpet (1 Cor. 15:50-52; Rev. 11:15). Their bodies will be instantly transformed.

reprobate: The Tribulation will be a unique time in history because billions will become reprobate, as is seen by their taking the mark of the Beast. A reprobate person is one who has no desire at all to repent (Rom. 1:28; Heb. 6:4, 2 Pet. 2:20). After the Tribulation begins, the saints will continue to pray for mercy for the lost, but will add the unique dimension of praying for judgment on the reprobate who will not repent and who will continue to violently oppress and kill the saints (Rev. 19:2). We join with the prayers of the martyrs in the fifth seal, praying that the oppression caused by the reprobate would be stopped by the judgment of God.

replacement theology: An unbiblical teaching stating that the Jews have been permanently rejected by God and have thus been replaced by the Church as the true Israel, which now inherits the national promises that God gave to the nation of Israel (Rom. 9-11).

restrainer: The restrainer peaks of that which restrains the Antichrist. It will be taken out of the way to allow him to come to a place of international political power. This restraining force refers to a combination of two forces referred to by Paul as someone and something that now restrains the Antichrist (2 Thes. 2:6-8). Paul described the restrainer of the Antichrist as a "what" (neuter in v. 6) and as a "He" (masculine in v. 7). Thus, the restraining force is a "what" and a "He" working together. Paul taught that the power of the state is appointed by God to restrain evil (Rom. 13:1-4). The "what" that restrains the Antichrist is the power of the state; the "He" is God and His sovereign decree related to the timing in which the restraints on the Antichrist are lifted. Some wrongly teach that the Holy Spirit is the restrainer and that He is removed when the Church is raptured before the Tribulation. If that were true, then no one could be saved in the Tribulation, because it takes the work of the Holy Spirit moving on an unbeliever's heart for them to be saved.

second coming of Christ: The time when Jesus will come back physically to Jerusalem to rule the whole earth. He will travel across the earth in the sky so that every eye will clearly see Him in every nation of the earth (Rev. 1:7).

second coming procession: The three-stage process of the return of Jesus, traveling first across the sky so that every eye will see Him (Rev. 1:7), then through the land of Edom, which is modern-day Jordan (Isa. 63:1-6; Hab. 3:3-16), as He marches up to Jerusalem to the Mount of Olives (Ps. 24:7-10; Zech. 14:4 ; Rev. 19:17-21).

seven heads: Seven vast empires throughout history that persecuted Israel. They are the empires of Egypt, Assyria, Babylon, Persia, Greece, ancient Rome, and a still-future, revived Roman Empire (Dan. 2:41-42; 7:7, 20, 24; Rev. 12:3; 13:1; 17:3-16).

ten horns: A future, ten-nation confederation of ten kings who rule simultaneously over their own nations. They come into an enthusiastic agreement or partnership together under the Antichrist's authority (Dan. 2:41-42; 7:7, 20, 24; 11:36-45; Rev. 12:3; 13:1; 17:3, 7, 12, 16).

thirty-day period: In Daniel 12:11, an angel told Daniel about a thirty-day period that would extend beyond the commonly understood 1,260 days (three and a half years) in which God supernaturally provides for the remnant of Israel (Rev. 12:6, 14), the two witnesses prophesy (Rev. 11:3), and the Antichrist persecutes the saints (Rev. 13:5). This period of 1,260 days ends when Jesus comes in the sky at the seventh trumpet to rapture the saints (Rev. 11:17). The 1,290 days speak of an additional thirty days after the seventh trumpet in which the Antichrist's worship system or the abomination of desolation continues on earth. It ends when Jesus marches into Jerusalem to personally destroy the Antichrist (2 Thes. 2:8; Rev. 19:20).

throne of glory: Jesus will establish His throne of glory on earth in the Jerusalem temple (Jer. 3:17; Mt. 25:31-32) where it will be connected to the Holy of Holies in the temple during the Millennium (Ezek. 43:4-7; Zech. 6:12-13). Jesus' throne will connect heaven and earth together since His one throne is also located in the New Jerusalem, which descends to the earth above earthly Jerusalem during the millennial kingdom (Ps. 48:1-6; Rev. 22:3).

three and a half years: The Antichrist will be given authority to continue against Israel and the Church for 42 months. (Rev. 13:5). The Gentiles, under his leadership, will oppress Jerusalem for 42 months (Rev. 11:2). The two witnesses prophesy in Jerusalem for 1,260 days (Rev. 11:3). The remnant of Israel will be hidden from the Antichrist in the wilderness for 1,260 days (Rev. 12:6), also described as time, times, and half a time (Rev. 12:14). The Antichrist will be given authority to continue against the saints for time, times, and half a time, or three and a half years (Dan. 7:25). Israel's strength will be completely shattered after three and a half years (time, times, and half a time, Dan. 12:7). The term *time* refers to one year, *times* refers to two years and *half a time* means half a year (2 Thes. 2:3-12; 1 Jn. 2:18, 22; Rev. 13:1-18).

Tribulation/Great Tribulation: Some refer to the Tribulation as the entire seven-year period leading up to Jesus' return. However, Jesus specifically referred to the last three and a half years of that seven-year period as the Great Tribulation (Mt. 24:21, 29; Mk. 13:24; Rev. 7:14). It is also referred to as the time of Jacob's trouble (Jer. 30:4-7). The main focus of the Great Tribulation is the release of God's judgments on the Antichrist. These judgments will be released through the praying Church on earth (Rev. 6-19). The saints will not come under God's judgments but will be the ones releasing them on the Antichrist, just as Moses released God's judgments on Pharaoh (Ex. 7-12). A secondary theme of the Great Tribulation is the Antichrist's persecution of the saints.

two witnesses: Two prophets who will operate in the power of God in a remarkable way during the Great Tribulation (Rev. 11:3-6). They will oppose the Antichrist and proclaim the message of the gospel. Although their actual identities are unknown, some speculate that they are Moses and Elijah, or possibly Moses and Enoch.

MORE RESOURCES BY MIKE BICKLE

The Book of Revelation series
Available on CD, DVD, and MP3

The First Commandment series
Available on CD, DVD, and MP3

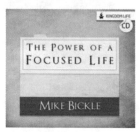

The Power of a Focused Life series
Available on CD and MP3

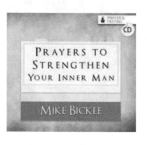

Prayers to Strengthen Your Inner Man series
Available on CD, DVD, and MP3

Visit MikeBickle.org for free resources

ORDER OF KEY EVENTS: THREE PROPHETIC TIME FRAMES

There are three basic time frames in God's end-time purpose:

First time frame: beginning of birth pangs (1948-?)—wars and rumors of wars (Mt. 24:4-8). This is the time that I believe we are currently in. In this time frame, there will be great turmoil in the nations with wars and rumors of wars, plus famines, pestilences, and earthquakes. My first option is to see this period beginning in 1948, when Israel became a nation. My second option is to see it beginning in 1967, when Jerusalem came under Israel's authority.

Second time frame: increased labor pangs (first three and a half years)—counterfeit world peace (1 Thes. 5:3; 2 Thes. 2:3). Paul prophesied of the time when many will say "peace and safety." A solution will seemingly be found to end the time of terrorism, wars, and rumors of wars. The Antichrist will bring a counterfeit and temporary world peace by confirming a covenant that will affect many nations, especially in the Middle East (Dan. 9:27). By doing this, he will be "revealed" on the world stage as a man of peace (2 Thes. 2:3). At this time, the harlot Babylon worldwide religion will prosper on a global scale, yet will persecute the saints (Mt. 24:9-14; Rev. 17:1-6), causing some believers to falling away from the faith (2 Thes. 2:3; 1 Tim. 4:1). All these things will occur during the first three and a half years of the final seven years that lead to Jesus' second coming.

Third time frame: hard labor pangs (final three and a half years)—Great Tribulation (Mt. 24:21; Rev. 6-19).
Chronological section #1: seal judgments (Rev. 6). At the first seal, the Antichrist is unveiled as a man of sin who begins to conquer (Rev. 6:1-2). The harlot Babylon religion will be destroyed by the ten kings who will work closely with the Antichrist (Rev. 17:16). The Antichrist's religion of intolerance will replace the Babylon religion. All will be forced by the threat of death to worship the Antichrist, who will set up his image in the Jerusalem temple which begins the abomination of desolation (Mt. 24:15; 2 Thes. 2:4; Rev. 13:4-18).
Chronological section #2: trumpet judgments (Rev. 8-9)
Chronological section #3: Jesus' second coming procession begins with the rapture (1 Cor. 15:52; Rev. 11:15)
Chronological section #4: bowl judgments (Rev. 15-16) Bowls will be poured out as Jesus marches through Edom to Jerusalem (Isa. 63:1-6; Hab. 3:3-13). The fall of the Babylon as a worldwide economic network (Rev. 18).
Chronological section #5: Jesus' triumphal entry into Jerusalem (Rev. 19:11-20:10)
  • Antichrist defeated at the battle of Jerusalem to end the Armageddon campaign
  • Millennial kingdom (Rev. 20:1-10)
  • New heaven, new earth (Rev. 21-22)

OVERVIEW OF KEY END TIME EVENTS

BROAD DAY OF THE LORD (2 Pet. 3:8-12): *From the Great Tribulation to the end of the Millennium*

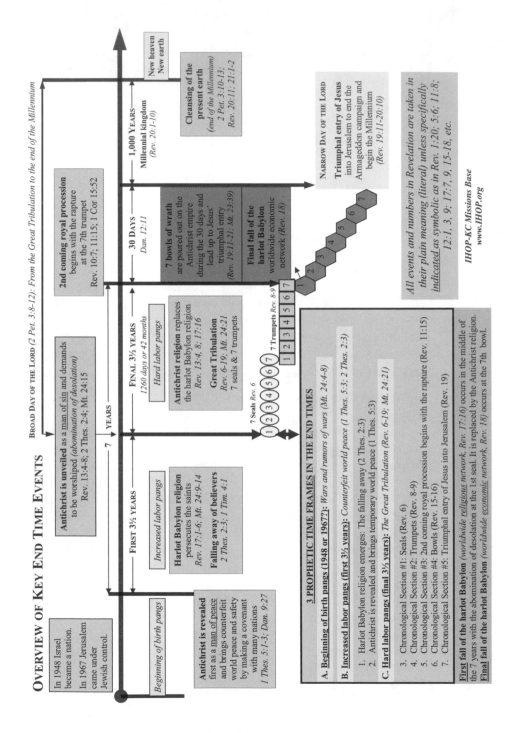

In 1948 Israel became a nation.
In 1967 Jerusalem came under Jewish control.

Beginning of birth pangs

Antichrist is revealed first as a man of peace and brings counterfeit world peace and safety by making a covenant with many nations
1 Thes. 5:1-3; Dan. 9:27

Antichrist is unveiled as a man of sin and demands to be worshiped (*abomination of desolation*)
Rev. 13:4-8; 2 Thes. 2:4; Mt. 24:15

FIRST 3½ YEARS

Increased labor pangs

Harlot Babylon religion persecutes the saints
Rev. 17:1-6; Mt. 24:9-14
Falling away of believers
2 Thes. 2:3; 1 Tim. 4:1

— 7 — YEARS

FINAL 3½ YEARS
1260 days or 42 months

Hard labor pangs

Antichrist religion replaces the harlot Babylon religion
Rev. 13:4, 8; 17:16

Great Tribulation
Rev. 6-19; Mt. 24:21
7 seals & 7 trumpets

7 Seals *Rev. 6*
①②③④⑤⑥⑦

7 Trumpets *Rev. 8-9*
①②③④⑤⑥⑦

2nd coming royal procession begins with the rapture at the 7th trumpet
Rev. 10:7; 11:15; 1 Cor 15:52

30 DAYS
Dan. 12:11

7 bowls of wrath are poured out on the Antichrist empire during the 30 days and lead up to Jesus' triumphal entry
(Rev. 19:11-21; Mt. 23:39)

Final fall of the harlot Babylon worldwide economic network *(Rev. 18)*

1 2 3 4 5 6 7

NARROW DAY OF THE LORD

Triumphal entry of Jesus into Jerusalem to end the Armageddon campaign and begin the Millennium *(Rev. 19:11-20:10)*

1,000 YEARS
Millennial kingdom *(Rev. 20:1-10)*

New heaven
New earth

Cleansing of the present earth *(end of the Millennium)*
2 Pet. 3:10-13;
Rev. 20:11; 21:1-2

All events and numbers in Revelation are taken in their plain meaning (literal) unless specifically indicated as symbolic as in Rev. 1:20; 5:6; 11:8; 12:1, 3, 9; 17:7, 9, 15-18, etc.

IHOP-KC Missions Base
www.IHOP.org

---

3 PROPHETIC TIME FRAMES IN THE END TIMES

A. Beginning of birth pangs (1948 or 1967?): *Wars and rumors of wars (Mt. 24:4-8)*

B. Increased labor pangs (first 3½ years): *Counterfeit world peace (1 Thes. 5:3; 2 Thes. 2:3)*
1. Harlot Babylon religion emerges: The falling away (2 Thes. 2:3)
2. Antichrist is revealed and brings temporary world peace (1 Thes. 5:3)

C. Hard labor pangs (final 3½ years): *The Great Tribulation (Rev. 6-19; Mt. 24:21)*
3. Chronological Section #1: Seals (Rev. 6)
4. Chronological Section #2: Trumpets (Rev. 8-9)
5. Chronological Section #3: 2nd coming royal procession begins with the rapture (Rev. 11:15)
6. Chronological Section #4: Bowls (Rev. 15-16)
7. Chronological Section #5: Triumphal entry of Jesus into Jerusalem (Rev. 19)

First fall of the harlot Babylon (*worldwide religious network, Rev. 17:16*) occurs in the middle of the 7 years with the abomination of desolation at the 1st seal. It is replaced by the Antichrist religion. **Final fall of the harlot Babylon** (*worldwide economic network, Rev. 18*) occurs at the 7th bowl.

Jesus' Battle Plan in the Book of Revelation

FINAL 3½ YEARS   **GREAT TRIBULATION REV. 6-19**

1st Seal	2nd Seal	3rd Seal	4th Seal	5th Seal	6th Seal	7th Seal
Antichrist's political aggression	Bloodshed and final world war	Famine and economic crisis	1/4 of humanity is killed	Prayer strengthened by martyrs	Cosmic disturbances and God's glory	Prayer strengthened by angels

T R U M P E T S

| 1st Trumpet 1/3 of the earth's vegetation burns |
| 2nd Trumpet 1/3 of the sea turns to blood |
| 3rd Trumpet 1/3 of the fresh water becomes bitter |
| 4th Trumpet 1/3 of the sun, moon and stars are darkened |
| 5th Trumpet Demonic locusts torment 5 months |
| 6th Trumpet Demonic horsemen kill 1/3 of the earth |
| 7th Trumpet The rapture and the return of Jesus |

1st Bowl	2nd Bowl	3rd Bowl	4th Bowl	5th Bowl	6th Bowl	7th Bowl
Loathsome sores on the Antichrist worshipers	The sea turns to blood killing the sea life	The earth's fresh water turns to blood	Men are scorched with great heat by the sun	Painful darkness on the Antichrist's empire	Deceiving the nations to come to Armageddon	Earthquakes, hail, and the final fall of Babylon

30 Days (Dan. 12:11)

The 7 bowls are poured out as Jesus marches across the land through Jordan to Jerusalem (Isa. 63:1-6; Hab. 3:3-13; Ps. 110:5-7; 45:3-5)

Triumphal entry of Jesus into Jerusalem

to end the Armageddon campaign (Rev. 19:11-21)

2nd coming royal procession over 30 days in 3 stages (*Dan. 12:11*): *begins with the 7th Trumpet (Rev.11:15; 1 Cor. 15:52; 1 Thes. 4:16)*

1. **Procession in the sky worldwide:** *Rapture (Mt. 24:30-31; Rev. 1:7)*
2. **Procession across the land:** *Through Jordan to Jerusalem (Isa. 63:1-6; Hab. 3:3-13; Ps. 110:5-7; 45:3-5)*
3. **Procession into Jerusalem (Mount of Olives):** *Triumphal entry of Jesus into Jerusalem to end the Armageddon campaign (Mt. 23:39; Ps. 24:7-10; Rev. 19:11-21)*

3 types of people on earth (*at the time of the rapture*)
1. **Redeemed:** Raptured at the start of the second coming procession
2. **Reprobate:** Took the mark of the Beast (they will be killed)
3. **Resisters:** Are the unsaved survivors of the tribulation who refused to worship the Antichrist. The Scripture refers to them as "those who are left" or "who remain." These will have an opportunity to be converted after Jesus returns. They will then populate the millennial earth (Isa. 4:3; 10:20; 11:11; 49:6; 65:8; 66:19; Jer. 31:2; Ezek. 20:38-42; 36:36; Dan. 12:1; Amos 9:5-10; Joel 2:32; Zech. 12:14; 13:8; 14:16).

OUTLINE OF REVELATION: 4 MAIN PARTS

Pt 1 Rev. 1: John's calling to prophesy on the end times
Pt 2 Rev. 2-3: Jesus' 7 letters to 7 churches
Pt 3 Rev. 4-5: Jesus takes the scroll from the Father
Pt 4 Rev. 6-22: Jesus' battle plan to cleanse the earth
(Pt 4 has 5 chronological sections & 5 angelic explanations)

* **5 Chronological sections:** Jesus' battle plan to cleanse the earth by judging the Antichrist systems (Seals, Trumpets, Bowls)

* **5 Angelic explanations:** John gains perspective from angels on why the judgments are so severe and what happens to the saints

Rev. 6   **Chronological Section #1: Seal judgments**
Rev. 7   Angelic Explanation #1: Protection

Rev. 8-9   **Chronological Section #2: Trumpet judgments**
Rev. 10-11   Angelic Explanation #2: Direction

Rev. 11:15   **Chronological Section #3: Second Coming**
Rev. 12-14   Angelic Explanation #3: Confrontation

Rev. 15-16   **Chronological Section #4: Bowl judgments**
Rev. 17-18   Angelic Explanation #4: Seduction

Rev. 19:11-21:8   **Chron. Section #5: Triumphal entry** *of Jesus into Jerusalem to begin the Millennium and then the new earth*
Rev. 21:9-22:5   Angelic Explanation #5: Restoration